THE
CHRIST
WE KNEW

THE
CHRIST
WE KNEW

EYEWITNESS ACCOUNTS FROM
MATTHEW, MARK, LUKE, AND JOHN

WITH 31 DAYS OF DEVOTIONS BY
CALVIN MILLER

Featuring the Holman Christian Standard Bible

HOLMAN
BIBLE PUBLISHERS

Nashville, Tennessee

DEDICATION

To the translation team in general,

To Arthur Farstad,
who having departed to be with God,
nonetheless began this dream,

To Ed Blum,
the chief translator whose scholarship
ever pulls the vision into wholeness,

To David Shepherd,
for his pursuit of excellence,

But mostly,
To Hansie and Betsy,
for their day-to-day walk of faith.

CONTENTS

INTRODUCTION

The Word of God! What is it? What glory its origins? What hope its destiny? Scrolls, vellums, papyrus, ink, and time! The first real light of morning, the last warmth of presence at midnight – light from the ancient past made to shine on today's complexities – the unforsaking word from the unforsaking God. All this is the Bible. Rapture and instruction gather round God's revelation of Himself.

This last year I joined David Shepherd and John Perry – both fellow stylists – and a host of translators headed up by Dr. Ed Blum of Dallas Theological Seminary to begin work on the Holman Christian Standard Bible. I had no idea how Bible translation teams really worked, but the experience has proved to be exhilarating. I've found poring over hundreds of pages of text and translation to be most rewarding. No, more than that – it's transforming. It is impossible to work on ancient texts with the intention of bringing God's clear word to Christians everywhere without feeling that in the labor lies something of the reason one is born. My prayer is that the Holman Christian Standard Bible may become a life-long, love affair for multiplied believers.

I am not a translator. My knowledge of Greek and Hebrew is respectable but far from good enough to be official. I suspect I was selected to be a part of this team not because I know the ancient languages, but because I know English fairly well. It was my desire to see what my small area of expertise might add to those scholars who do know and read the ancient manuscripts. At best I have offered merely English counsel on how to make each translated sentence as readable and riveting as it might be.

But "pretty" is not all it takes to make a translation. Integrity and ancient word meanings must ever remain in place. To accomplish this I have found great joy in working with the "doctors" who really know the ancient manuscripts.

So I have lived with the English words of the Bible – I have prayed over those words – that I might give the Hebrew and Greek words the best chance to have a good English life. I have baptized every word in the sweat of my intention. I have blessed the drudgery and sanctified the long hours of work. I have come to know what Suzanne Harvey meant when she said:

> "Every word's dipped in blood,
> Marinated in sweat, seasoned with doubt . . .
> You enshrine a semicolon,
> Canonize a verb,
> Beatify some errant phrase,
> When the seconds stretch like rubber bands
> Then snap, boomerang and ricochet,
> Hurling you back on the blank page.

Every sentence is etched in acid
We chisel from the marrow of our bones."

So working on this translation has been a chiseling from my bones, an effort agonized over my utter concern for English readability. Yet never once have I tried to call attention to the words I've helped select. I agree with Andrew Wyeth who said that our craft should never be exhibitionist. Rather "the craft should be submerged . . . rightfully the handmaiden of beauty, power and emotional content."[1]

When Martin Luther was asked how he preached to intellectuals like Philip Melancthon who thronged to his great congregation, he answered in this way: "When I preach, I preach to Hansie and Betsy. If they understand, so will the theologians present."[2] In my stylistic work I must confess I have thought mostly of how this new Bible would sound to Hansie and Betsy. I wanted the scholarship to be right, but I have always worshiped the God who hides Himself from the wise and reveals Himself unto babes.

Let's face it. Life is not easy for Hansie and Betsy. They rise early, work hard, suffer from family problems. They know sickness and dying. They know job loss, desperation, and the specter of futility, depression, and terminal illness. Hansie and Betsy sometimes have good days, but they have learned even on those days to pick up the Book. For God has something to say to them that will make their lives livable and their hopes bloom eternal.

The original Hansie and Betsy have slept these past four centuries in a German graveyard awaiting all that the Book promised them while they were alive. But the Hansie and Betsy I hope I have served in this translation are still with us, and they need God and his Word to get through the day. I have toiled over the words of this translation to help them. But I don't want Hansie and Betsy to see this as a nice translation. If that's how they see it, they will not read it for long. No, my prayer is that Hansie and Betsy will select this Book to be their Bible. I pray it will be God's Word specifically for them. May they go in tears to this Book. May they hurry into its pages – by sun and candlelight – to find answers for their brokenness, a balm for the ache of their times.

But to you dear, Hansie and Betsy, I must confess: We are much alike. Your struggles are mine! What this translation team has done, it has done for both of us. Still, I want this to be your Book, your compass in Canaan – your guide to a city built foursquare – your own special map for your own special God-Trek! Most of all, I want this – your own special Book – to help you know Christ better. After all, His gospels throb with our salvation. He is a Christ who will never leave us or forsake us – a Christ who is the same yesterday and forever.

That's why this volume you're holding today, which focuses on the life and witness of our Lord Jesus Christ, carries such particular importance to me. Long have I labored through words and images to make Him known more clearly, to capture unnoticed aspects of His presence and character, and to paint them in colors not found on the primary palette. Long have I sought to convey the reaction of those who actually felt the fabric of His robe brush their arm or stood stunned and silent before His penetrating gaze. Long have I pleaded with my imagination to extend its tireless search onto trackless ground, to battle the fatigue of lifeless form and familiarity in order to show Jesus to those who think cursory knowledge is enough to satisfy their curiosity.

This book, which knits the events of Christ's life into one seamless storyline, is my own attempt to help you see Him afresh – through scenes that date back centuries yet somehow share a seat in the chair right next to you.

So, here's to you, Hansie and Betsy, dear sisters in life's struggles. This is not just another book, not just another Bible translation! This is the Book—your Book! Let it deepen your love affair with God and His Son! Study it and learn who you are and where you came from. Delve into its depths and find your destiny. Savor it in sour moments and find sweetness, in weak moments and be strong. It's all for you, Hansie and Betsy! Read and grow rich!

CALVIN MILLER
Birmingham, Alabama
March 2000

[1] Fred W. Mueser, Luther the Preacher (Minneapolis: Augsburg, 1983), 114.
[2] Fred W. Mueser, Luther the Preacher (Minneapolis: Augsburg, 1983), 35

INTRODUCING
THE HOLMAN CHRISTIAN STANDARD BIBLE

Bible study is the road God's people take to hear and obey our Creator and Savior. The Holman Christian Standard Bible™ offers believers in the third millennium an up-to-date translation designed specifically for the needs of students of Scripture. It seeks to provide a translation as close to the words of the Hebrew and Greek texts as possible while still maintaining the literary quality and ease of reading that invite and enable people to read, study, and obey God's Word. To reach God's people effectively, a translation must provide a reverent, exalted text that is also within reach of its readers.

Translating the Bible in English offers a double challenge. First, each language has its own vocabulary, grammar, and syntax that cannot be rendered exactly into another language. Second, contemporary culture so honors relativism and individual freedom that it distrusts claims to absolute authority.

PRECISION WITH CLARITY

The first challenge means that English translators must avoid creating a special form of the language that does not communicate well to modern readers. For example, John 1:6 in Greek reads, "was a man having been sent from God, name to him John." The English translator must provide a word order and syntax that follow the dynamics of the English language and that are familiar to English readers. In this instance, the Holman Christian Standard Bible reads, "There was a man named John who was sent from God." This accurately represents the Greek text but also presents it in a form readers should find inviting and natural.

On the other hand, the Holman Christian Standard Bible is not based on a theory of translation that considers completely dispensable the form of the original language. Rules governing word order are very different in Hebrew, Greek, and English. But English shares with Hebrew and Greek certain grammatical forms such as nouns, verbs, prepositional phrases, independent and dependent clauses, and so forth. In most cases these forms perform similar functions in English as they do in Hebrew or Greek. Therefore, since grammatical form is one way that language communicates, we have retained the grammatical form of the original whenever it can be rendered into English with sufficient accuracy and clarity. Nevertheless, this is not a strict word-for-word translation since it is often impossible to render one and only one English word for every Hebrew or Greek word. Language differences often require several English words to render one Hebrew or Greek word, and sometimes a Hebrew or Greek phrase may be more accurately and clearly translated by one word in English.

COMMUNICATING WITH AUTHORITY

The second challenge, that of contemporary culture, means translators must hold firm to traditional beliefs about the authority of Scripture and avoid modern temptations to rewrite the Bible to say what modern readers want to hear. Translators must remember that the divine Author of the Bible inspired His Word for people today and for all time just as much as for the original audience. The Holman Christian Standard Bible stands on the authority of God and has attempted to provide an accurate and readable translation of the Greek text. The mission of the Holman Christian Standard Bible is to produce as precise a translation of the Hebrew, Aramaic, and Greek Scriptures as possible with the use of newly-published lexicons, grammars, and computer programs. The goal of this kind of translation is to encourage in-depth Bible study, but this translation also seeks to be highly readable (for public and private use) and also useful for personal memorization.

THE MAKINGS OF A NEW TRANSLATION

With these goals in view, an international and interdenominational team of more than eighty scholars has been formed to translate the Scriptures from the original languages. This translation project is being undertaken by Holman Bible Publishers, the oldest Bible publisher in America. Its origin can be traced back to a Philadelphia firm founded by Christopher Sower in 1743. Holman is spiritually grounded in the belief that the Bible is inerrant and is the sole authority for faith and practice in the life of a Christian.

In order to produce this translation, Holman Bible Publishers entered into a partnership with Dr. Art Farstad, former General

Editor of the New King James Version. Art had been working on a new translation of the Bible for several years when in the Spring of 1998 he agreed to contract with Holman to complete the project. Art served as General Editor of this translation project until his death on September 1, 1998. His Assistant Editor and coworker, Dr. Ed Blum, former professor at Dallas Theological Seminary, picked up the mantle of leadership that Art left behind and now serves as General Editor of the Holman Christian Standard Bible.

HOW TO ENJOY THIS EDITION

This presentation of the Gospels deliberately avoids using some standard features found in other editions of the Holman Christian Standard Bible – namely, footnotes and other explanatory material designed to enhance deeper study. *The Christ We Knew* is not intended to be used as a study Bible. Here, the precise clarity of the Holman Christian Standard Bible is yours simply to read, receive, and enjoy.

This quality is an important one because, despite a person's need to explore the depths of a Bible word or passage, to weigh its textual variants and consider its historical context, the higher purpose in reading the Scriptures is to relate to the God of the Bible. Both scholar and student alike must ultimately approach the Bible with all other devices laid to rest, with no more noble intent than meeting with God through His Son, Jesus Christ.

The Holman Christian Standard Bible has been carefully, meticulously crafted with this very purpose in mind, so that the hard work of biblical translation might result in the simple joy of personal Bible reading. Find in this harmonious retelling of the life of Christ the many reasons you call Him Lord, the many reasons you long to worship and serve Him.

*S*ince many have undertaken to compile a narrative about the events that have been fulfilled among us, just as the original eyewitnesses and servants of the word handed them down to us, it also seemed good to me, having carefully investigated everything from the very first, to write to you in orderly sequence, most honorable Theophilus, so that you may know the certainty of the things about which you have been instructed.

—THE GOSPEL OF LUKE
CHAPTER 1, VERSES 1-4

The boy grew up and became strong, filled with wisdom, and God's grace was on Him. . . . And Jesus increased in wisdom and stature and in favor with God and with people.

The Adolescent Messiah
LUKE 2:40,52

We all know the story of Christ's birth. We sing it, we celebrate it, we wonder at the mystery of it. But Jesus grew. He expressed a hungering to get wiser, bigger, and better at relationships—both his relationship with his Father in heaven and his relationships with those around him.

First, Jesus grew in wisdom. The heart of Jesus' wisdom may gather itself about the Sermon on the Mount. In this most famous sermon ever preached, the appeal is not to get smarter as a Ph.D. might but to learn the lessons of the lilies, the birds, the wise and foolish builders. At the end of this sermon, Matthew makes this comment: "When Jesus had finished this sermon, the crowds were astonished at His teaching. For He was teaching them like one who had authority, and not like their scribes." (Mt 7:28-29). There is no substitute for growing in wisdom.

Jesus also grew in stature. What baby does not want to be a child? What child does not want to be an adolescent? What adolescent does not long to be a man or a woman? There can be no doubt that Jesus wanted to grow up. One very famous psychologist said that most people get full grown in their bodies, but they remain adolescent in their temperaments all their lives. Not so with Jesus. He matured in every way.

He also grew in favor with God. Jesus had a longing to know God, to be with God. His prayer life reflected his appetite to be one with God. He walked and talked with God so his bonding with his Father would be a growing and dependent relationship. He knew God to be his Father, and he passed this glorious "Abba" word on to the rest of us.

Finally, Jesus grew in favor with people. He liked people, both those who liked him and those who didn't. No one was beyond the scope of his desire to love. He reached from the cross to prove he was the greatest person who ever lived.

Jesus considered maturity the business of every believer. Do you? Are you growing in wisdom and in your love affair with God and humanity?

PRAYER
Lord, I want to grow. I never want to stop growing! I want my maturity to be a gift that I give you to make you as attractive as I can to others and to be able to make your influence optimal in my minimal world.

CHAPTER ONE

THE BIRTH OF JESUS

In those days a decree went out from Caesar Augustus that the whole empire should be registered. [2] This first registration took place while Quirinius was governing Syria. [3] So everyone went to be registered, each to his own town.

[4] And Joseph also went up from the town of Nazareth in Galilee, to Judea, to the city of David, which is called Bethlehem, because he was of the house and family line of David, [5] to be registered along with Mary, who was engaged to him and was pregnant. [6] While they were there, it happened that the days were completed for her to give birth. [7] Then she gave birth to her firstborn Son, and she wrapped Him snugly in cloth and laid Him in a manger—because there was no room for them at the inn.

THE SHEPHERDS AND THE ANGELS

[8] In the same region, shepherds were living out in the fields and keeping watch at night over their flock.

⁹ Then an angel of the Lord stood before them, and the glory of the Lord shone around them, and they were terrified. ¹⁰ But the angel said to them, "Do not be afraid, for you see, I announce to you good news of great joy, which will be for all the people: ¹¹ because today in the city of David was born for you a Savior, who is Christ the Lord. ¹² This will be the sign for you: you will find a baby wrapped snugly in cloth and lying in a manger."

¹³ Suddenly there was a multitude of the heavenly host with the angel, praising God and saying:

¹⁴ "Glory to God in the highest heaven,

and peace on earth to people He favors!"

¹⁵ When the angels had left them and returned to heaven, the shepherds said to one another, "Let's go straight to Bethlehem and see this thing that has taken place, which the Lord has made known to us."

¹⁶ And they hurried off and found both Mary and Joseph, and the baby who was lying in the manger. ¹⁷ After seeing them, they reported the message they were told about this child, ¹⁸ and all who heard it were amazed at what the shepherds said to them. ¹⁹ But Mary was treasuring up all these things in her heart and meditating on them. ²⁰ The shepherds returned, glorifying and praising God for all they had seen and heard, just as they had been told.

THE CIRCUMCISION AND PRESENTATION OF JESUS

²¹ When the eight days were completed for His circumcision, He was named JESUS—the name given by the angel before He was

conceived. ²² And when the days of their purification according to the law of Moses were completed, they brought Him up to Jerusalem to present Him to the Lord ²³ (just as it is written in the law of the Lord: "Every firstborn male will be called holy to the Lord") ²⁴ and to offer a sacrifice (according to what is stated in the law of the Lord: "a pair of turtledoves or two young pigeons").

SIMEON'S PROPHETIC PRAISE

²⁵ There was a man in Jerusalem whose name was Simeon. This man was righteous and devout, looking forward to Israel's consolation, and the Holy Spirit was upon him. ²⁶ It had been revealed to him by the Holy Spirit that he would not see death before he saw the Lord's Messiah. ²⁷ Guided by the Spirit, he entered the temple complex. When the parents brought in the child Jesus to perform for Him what was customary under the law, ²⁸ Simeon took Him up in his arms, praised God, and said:

> ²⁹ "Now, Master, You can dismiss Your slave in peace,
> according to Your word.
> ³⁰ For my eyes have seen Your salvation,
> ³¹ which You have prepared in the presence of all
> peoples;
> ³² a light for revelation to the Gentiles
> and glory to Your people Israel."

³³ His father and mother were amazed at what was being said about Him. ³⁴ Then Simeon blessed them and told His mother Mary: "Indeed, this child is destined to cause the fall and rise of many in Israel, and to be a sign that will be opposed—and a sword

will pierce your own soul—that the thoughts of many hearts may be revealed."

ANNA'S TESTIMONY

[36] There was also a prophetess, Anna, a daughter of Phanuel, of the tribe of Asher. She was well along in years, having lived with a husband seven years after her marriage, [37] and was a widow for eighty-four years. She did not leave the temple complex, serving God night and day with fastings and prayers. [38] At that very moment, she came up and began to thank God and to speak about Him to all who were looking forward to the redemption of Jerusalem.

THE FAMILY'S RETURN TO NAZARETH

[39] When they had completed everything according to the law of the Lord, they returned to Galilee, to their own town of Nazareth. [40] The boy grew up and became strong, filled with wisdom, and God's grace was on Him.

IN HIS FATHER'S HOUSE

[41] Every year His parents traveled to Jerusalem for the Passover Festival. [42] When He was twelve years old, they went up according to the custom of the festival. [43] After those days were over, as they were returning, the boy Jesus stayed behind in Jerusalem, but His parents did not know it. [44] Assuming He was in the traveling party, they went a day's journey. Then they began looking for Him among

their relatives and friends. 45 When they did not find Him, they returned to Jerusalem to search for Him. 46 After three days, they found Him in the temple complex sitting among the teachers, listening to them and asking them questions. 47 And all those who heard Him were astounded at His understanding and His answers. 48 When his parents saw Him, they were astonished, and His mother said to Him, "Son, why have You treated us like this? Here Your father and I have been anxiously searching for You."

49 "Why were you searching for Me?" He asked them. "Didn't you know that I must be involved in my Father's interests?" 50 But they did not understand what He said to them.

IN FAVOR WITH GOD AND WITH PEOPLE

51 Then He went down with them and came to Nazareth, and was obedient to them. His mother kept all these things in her heart. 52 And Jesus increased in wisdom and stature and in favor with God and with people.

The next day John saw Jesus coming toward him and said, "Here is the Lamb of God, who takes away the sin of the world!"

Behold the Lamb
JOHN 1:29

The Lamb of God! So John the Baptist greeted Jesus. This greeting referring to his sacrificial purpose must have become a memorable mark for Christ. Here publicly at the outset of his ministry, Jesus was reminded of all that would befall him at the end of his ministry.

John's greeting not only reminded Jesus about how his life would end. It also reminded him of the universal scope of his life: He would die for the sins of the whole world. The marvel of Jesus' life is that though he never forgot his worldwide significance, he was never grandiose about who he was. *Humility* is the word which best describes his all-important life. Humility for us is acquired by standing next to Christ and thus remembering our place. Jesus' humility had to come from keeping in touch with God and remembering how much God loves everyone.

Knowing his universal significance, Jesus still walked with ordinary people. He found time, even on the busiest days, to play with children. Knowing he would die, he still attended dinner parties. Divine Savior he was, and yet he used his divinity to minister to needy people. He fed the hungry, healed the lepers.

Still, his primary mission was to die. He is the Lamb of God—*Agnus Dei*, as Jerome had it. He would die. For all the wonderful things he would do while living, history forever after would not think of his name without thinking of his death. At the mere mention or thought of his name, the first thing people would think of would be his cross.

Still, he was young. While he would die young, this first public greeting would help him remember the entire reason for his incarnation. He was literally born to die. The only real reason for you to be born is to accept Jesus' sacrifice and to find your place in his service. The only reason for you to be born is to die to yourself—to take up your cross and follow him. You must live the dying life that he taught you. Your reason for being in the world will never become obvious to others until you "consider yourselves dead to sin, but alive to God in Christ Jesus" (Rm 6:11).

PRAYER

Lord, you were the Lamb of God from the very outset of your ministry. All the meaning that can be had in life came because you were willing not just to die for me, but to die to all self-interest. The same requirement is made of me. May I die to self that I may forever be alive in Christ.

CHAPTER TWO

PROLOGUE

In the beginning was the Word,
and the Word was with God,
and the Word was God.

2 He was with God in the beginning.

3 All things were created through Him,
and apart from Him not one thing
was created that has been created.

4 In Him was life,
and that life was the light of men.

5 That light shines in the darkness,
yet the darkness did not overcome it.

6 There was a man named John
who was sent from God.

7 He came as a witness
to testify about the light,
so that all might believe through him.

8 He was not the light,
but he came to testify about the light.

⁹ The true light, who gives light to everyone,
was coming into the world.

¹⁰ He was in the world,
and the world was created through Him,
yet the world did not know Him.

¹¹ He came to His own,
and His own people did not receive Him.

¹² But to all who did receive Him,
He gave them the right to be children of God,
to those who believe in His name,

¹³ who were born,
not of blood,
or of the will of the flesh,
or of the will of man,
but of God.

¹⁴ The Word became flesh
and took up residence among us.
We observed His glory,
the glory as the only Son from the Father,
full of grace and truth.

¹⁵ (John testified concerning Him and exclaimed,
"This was the One of whom I said,
'The One coming after me has surpassed me,
because He existed before me.' ")

¹⁶ For we have all received grace after grace
from His fullness.

¹⁷ For the law was given through Moses;

grace and truth came through Jesus Christ.

¹⁸ No one has ever seen God.

The only Son—

the One who is at the Father's side—

He has revealed Him.

JOHN THE BAPTIST'S TESTIMONY

¹⁹ This is John's testimony when the Jews from Jerusalem sent priests and Levites to ask him, "Who are you?"

²⁰ He confessed and did not deny, declaring, "I am not the Messiah."

²¹ "What then?" they asked him. "Are you Elijah?"

"I am not," he said.

"Are you the Prophet?"

"No," he answered.

²² "Who are you, then?" they asked. "We need to give an answer to those who sent us. What can you tell us about yourself?"

²³ He said, "I am 'A voice of one crying out in the wilderness: Make straight the way of the Lord'—just as Isaiah the prophet said."

²⁴ Now they had been sent from the Pharisees. ²⁵ So they asked him, "Why then do you baptize if you aren't the Messiah, or Elijah, or the Prophet?"

²⁶ "I baptize with water," John answered them. "But among you stands Someone you don't know. ²⁷ He is the One coming after me, whose sandal strap I'm not worthy to untie."

²⁸ All this happened in Bethany across the Jordan, where John was baptizing.

THE LAMB OF GOD

[29] The next day John saw Jesus coming toward him and said, "Here is the Lamb of God, who takes away the sin of the world! [30] This is the One I told you about: 'After me comes a man who has surpassed me, because He existed before me.' [31] I didn't know Him, but I came baptizing with water so He might be revealed to Israel."

[32] And John testified, "I watched the Spirit descending from heaven like a dove, and He rested upon Him. [33] I didn't know Him, but He who sent me to baptize with water told me, 'The One on whom you see the Spirit descending and resting—He is the One baptizing in the Holy Spirit.' [34] I have seen and testified that He is the Son of God!"

[35] Again the next day, John was standing with two of his disciples. [36] When he saw Jesus passing by, he said, "Look! The Lamb of God!"

[37] The two disciples heard him say this and followed Jesus. [38] When Jesus turned and noticed them following Him, He asked them, "What are you looking for?"

They said to Him, "Rabbi" (which means "Teacher"), "where are you staying?"

[39] "Come and you'll see," He replied. So they went and saw where He was staying, and they stayed with Him that day. It was about ten in the morning.

[40] Andrew, Simon Peter's brother, was one of the two who heard John and followed Him. [41] He first found his own brother Simon and told him, "We have found the Messiah!" (which means "Anointed One") [42] and brought him to Jesus.

When Jesus saw him, He said, "You are Simon, son of John. You will be called Cephas" (which means "Rock").

PHILIP AND NATHANAEL

[43] The next day He decided to leave for Galilee. Jesus found Philip and told him, "Follow Me!"

[44] Now Philip was from Bethsaida, the hometown of Andrew and Peter. [45] Philip found Nathanael and told him, "We have found the One of whom Moses wrote in the law (and so did the prophets): Jesus the son of Joseph, from Nazareth!"

[46] "Can anything good come out of Nazareth?" Nathanael asked him.

"Come and see," Philip answered.

[47] Then Jesus saw Nathanael coming toward Him and said about him, "Here is a true Israelite in whom is no deceit."

[48] "How do you know me?" Nathanael asked.

"Before Philip called you, when you were under the fig tree, I saw you," Jesus answered.

[49] "Rabbi," Nathanael replied, "You are the Son of God! You are the King of Israel!"

[50] Jesus responded to him, "Do you believe only because I told you I saw you under the fig tree? You will see greater things than this." [51] Then He said, "I assure you: You will see heaven opened and the angels of God ascending and descending upon the Son of Man."

When they heard this, all who were in the synagogue were enraged. They got up, drove Him out of town, and brought Him to the edge of the hill on which their town was built, intending to hurl Him over the cliff. But He passed right through the crowd and went on His way.

Negative Nazareth
LUKE 4:28-30

"Young Rabbi Killed after Hometown Sermon!" This could have been the headline of the Nazareth News, had there been a paper in that inhospitable place. The one person who would put Nazareth on the map was nearly martyred by his neighbors and friends. Jesus never went back to launch another Greater Nazarene Crusade. Jesus could do no mighty work there because of their lack of faith (see Mt 13:58).

The achievements of God are many and mighty, but this is only true if people actually believe that God can do mighty things. The power of God is omni-capable, but only where people believe that God can virtually do anything. The writer of Proverbs tells us that where there is no vision, the people perish (see Pr 29:18). It is equally true that where there is no faith, unbelieving people are inconsequential.

Nothing is more beautiful than people trying to accomplish some great thing in the name of Christ. These see themselves as weak, but we should never pity them. Those who hold any vision too great for them to accomplish on their own must rely on Jesus. For those are most blessed whom life reduces to such utter weakness that they cannot manage on their own. But watch the weak! See how they tremble and trust. What! Do these who have no strength still dream of conquering the stars? Yes. Their dream is reasonable, too. They have been made capable by his power.

Now let's talk about you. Do you tremble before the tasks that God has asked you to do? Remember Nazareth! You can doubt God, and nothing good will ever come out of your life. Or, you can believe, then watch what begins to happen. See the walls come down! Then count your weakness a blessing. It is because of your weakness that you pray for Christ to strengthen you. When you pray, you feel his wonderful power seeping into your frail intentions. Then your willpower starches its spine and stands to the task.

Thank God when you are terrified of all that he asks. Ask Christ to replace the terror with his power. Isn't it great to be doing the unbelievable? Get used to it. Outside of Nazareth, it is a way of life.

PRAYER
Lord, I wonder what you might do if I really believed.

CHAPTER THREE

THE TEMPTATION OF JESUS

Then Jesus returned from the Jordan, full of the Holy Spirit, and was led by the Spirit in the wilderness [2] for forty days to be tempted by the Devil. He ate nothing during those days, and when they were over, He was hungry. [3] The Devil said to Him, "If you are the Son of God, tell this stone to become bread."

[4] But Jesus answered him, "It is written: 'Man must not live on bread alone.'"

[5] So he took Him up and showed Him all the kingdoms of the world in a moment of time. [6] The Devil said to Him, "I will give You their splendor and all this authority, because it has been given over to me, and I can give it to anyone I want. [7] If You, then, will worship me, all will be Yours."

[8] And Jesus answered him, "It is written:

'You shall worship the Lord your God,
And Him alone you shall serve.'"

⁹ So he took Him to Jerusalem, had Him stand on the pinnacle of the temple, and said to Him, "If You are the Son of God, throw Yourself down from here. ¹⁰ For it is written:

> 'He will give His angels orders concerning you,
>
> to protect you,'
>
> and
>
> 'In their hands they will lift you up,
>
> so you will not strike your foot against a stone.'"

¹² And Jesus answered him, "It is said: 'You must not tempt the Lord your God.'"

¹³ After the Devil had finished every temptation, he departed from Him for a time.

MINISTRY IN GALILEE

¹⁴ Then Jesus returned to Galilee in the power of the Spirit, and news about Him spread throughout the entire vicinity. ¹⁵ He was teaching in their synagogues, being acclaimed by everyone.

REJECTION AT NAZARETH

¹⁶ He came to Nazareth, where He had been brought up. As usual, He entered the synagogue on the Sabbath day and stood up to read. ¹⁷ The scroll of the prophet Isaiah was given to Him, and unrolling the scroll, He found the place where it was written:

> ¹⁸ "The Spirit of the Lord is upon Me,
>
> because He has anointed Me
>
> to preach good news to the poor.
>
> He has sent Me to proclaim freedom to the captives

and recovery of sight to the blind,

to set free the oppressed,

¹⁹ to proclaim the year of the Lord's favor."

²⁰ He then rolled up the scroll, gave it back to the attendant, and sat down. And the eyes of everyone in the synagogue were fixed on Him. ²¹ He began by saying to them, "Today this Scripture has been fulfilled in your hearing."

²² They were all speaking well of Him and were amazed by the gracious words that came from His mouth, yet they said, "Isn't this Joseph's son?"

²³ Then He said to them, "No doubt you will quote this proverb to Me: 'Doctor, heal yourself.' 'All we've heard that took place in Capernaum, do here in your hometown also.' "

²⁴ He also said, "I assure you: No prophet is accepted in His hometown. ²⁵ But I say to you, there were certainly many widows in Israel in Elijah's days, when the sky was shut up for three years and six months while a great famine came over all the land. ²⁶ Yet Elijah was not sent to any of them, except to a widow at Zarephath in Sidon. ²⁷ And there were many lepers in Israel in the prophet Elisha's time, yet not one of them was cleansed except Naaman the Syrian."

²⁸ When they heard this, all who were in the synagogue were enraged. ²⁹ They got up, drove Him out of town, and brought Him to the edge of the hill on which their town was built, intending to hurl Him over the cliff. ³⁰ But He passed right through the crowd and went on His way.

DRIVING OUT AN UNCLEAN SPIRIT

[31] Then He went down to Capernaum, a town in Galilee, and was teaching them on the Sabbath. [32] And they were astonished at His teaching because His message had authority. [33] In the synagogue there was a man with an unclean demonic spirit who cried out with a loud voice, [34] "Leave us alone! What do You have to do with us, Jesus—Nazarene? Have You come to destroy us? I know who You are—the Holy One of God!"

[35] But Jesus rebuked him and said, "Be quiet and come out of him!"

And throwing him down before them, the demon came out of him without hurting him at all. [36] They were all struck with amazement and kept saying to one another, "What is this message? For with authority and power He commands the unclean spirits, and they come out!" [37] And news about Him began to go out to every place in the vicinity.

HEALINGS AT CAPERNAUM

[38] After He left the synagogue, He entered Simon's house. Simon's mother-in-law was suffering from a high fever, and they asked Him about her. [39] So He stood over her and rebuked the fever, and it left her. She got up immediately and began to serve them.

[40] When the sun was setting, all those who had anyone sick with various diseases brought them to Him. As He laid His hands on each

one of them, He would heal them. [41] Also, demons were coming out of many, shouting and saying, "You are the Son of God!" But He rebuked them and would not allow them to speak, because they knew He was the Messiah.

PREACHING IN GALILEE

[42] When it was day, He went out and made His way to a deserted place. But the crowds were searching for Him. They came to Him and tried to keep Him from leaving them. [43] But He said to them, "I must proclaim the good news about the kingdom of God to the other towns also, because I was sent for this purpose." [44] And He was preaching in the synagogues of Galilee.

No one sews a patch of unshrunk cloth on an old garment. Otherwise, the new patch pulls away from the old cloth, and a worse tear is made. And no one puts new wine into old wineskins. Otherwise, the wine will burst the skins, and the wine is lost as well as the skins. But new wine is for fresh wineskins.

Mending Old Clothes
MARK 2:21-22

Christianity is rooted in Judaism. The Messiah, the Christ, the Anointed One, is the fulfillment of Israel's millennial dream. So close are these two great faiths that many have wondered if there are any significant differences. So close are they that many misunderstandings have erupted because those outside of either faith expect that there should be no differences.

Jesus faced a huge dilemma. He wanted the Jews to turn in great numbers to the kingdom of God. At the same time, Jesus wanted all Jews to understand that the kingdom of God, as he preached it, was not a mere appendage to the ancient faith of Judaism. Christianity, which at that time had not even acquired the name, was to be a new, unique faith—distinct and separate.

The Law, the Ten Commandments, was the heart of Judaism. At the heart of the kingdom of God stands God's grace. These ways of relating to God were so separate in essence that they could in no way be merged. Jesus understood that many Jews would willingly become Christians if they could do so while leaving the bulk of Judaism intact. Jesus said that this could not happen.

Paul's letters made it clear that a great gulf existed between Judaism and Christianity. Gone would be the traditional Seder, even though the spirit of it might be preserved in the Lord's Supper. Gone, too, would be circumcision, a ritual at the heart of Jewish orthodoxy, although baptism would be the Christian ritual of belonging. Gone would be the ancient system of blood sacrifice, although Jesus' own blood would be celebrated as an all-encompassing sacrifice. Gone, too, would be all the Jewish holidays, although they would be replaced in time by Christian observances with awesome meaning.

From the outset, Jesus wanted all people to understand that God's new covenant of grace would welcome all people into a brand-new way of relating to God. Isn't it glorious that you are engulfed in this refreshing new way of worship? Have you thanked Jesus for these radical differences, so new in power and scope, that have the power to renovate your life?

PRAYER
Lord, I know that the whole of Christianity is to be characterized by the word "new." Why, then, do we so often look back to the good old days. They never were all that great. And besides, they keep us fondling old ideas that prevent us from moving into an exciting new future.

CHAPTER FOUR

THE SON OF MAN FORGIVES AND HEALS

When He entered Capernaum again after some days, it was reported that He was at home. ² So many people gathered together that there was no more room, even near the door, and He was speaking the message to them. ³ Then they came to Him bringing a paralytic, carried by four men. ⁴ Since they were not able to bring him to Jesus because of the crowd, they removed the roof above where He was. And when they had broken through, they lowered the stretcher on which the paralytic was lying.

⁵ Seeing their faith, Jesus told the paralytic, "Son, your sins are forgiven."

⁶ But some of the scribes were sitting there, reasoning in their hearts: ⁷ "Why does He speak like this? He's blaspheming! Who can forgive sins but God alone?"

⁸ Right away Jesus understood in His spirit that they were reasoning like this within themselves, and said

to them, "Why are you reasoning these things in your hearts? ⁹ Which is easier: to say to the paralytic, 'Your sins are forgiven,' or to say, 'Get up, pick up your stretcher and walk'? ¹⁰ But so you may know that the Son of Man has authority on earth to forgive sins," He told the paralytic, ¹¹ "I tell you: get up, pick up your stretcher, and go home."

¹² Immediately he got up, picked up the stretcher, and went out in front of everyone. As a result, they were all astounded and gave glory to God, saying, "We have never seen anything like this!"

THE CALL OF MATTHEW

¹³ Then Jesus went out again beside the sea. The whole crowd was coming to Him, and He taught them. ¹⁴ Then, moving on, He saw Levi the son of Alphaeus sitting at the tax office, and He said to him, "Follow Me!" So he got up and followed Him.

DINING WITH SINNERS

¹⁵ While He was reclining at the table in Levi's house, many tax collectors and sinners were also guests with Jesus and His disciples, because there were many who were following Him. ¹⁶ When the scribes of the Pharisees saw that He was eating with sinners and tax collectors, they asked His disciples, "Why does He eat with tax collectors and sinners?"

¹⁷ When Jesus heard this, He told them, "Those who are well don't need a doctor, but the sick do need one. I didn't come to call the righteous, but sinners."

A QUESTION ABOUT FASTING

¹⁸ Now John's disciples and the Pharisees were fasting. People came and asked Him, "Why do John's disciples and the Pharisees' disciples fast, but Your disciples do not fast?"

¹⁹ Jesus said to them, "The wedding guests cannot fast while the groom is with them, can they? As long as they have the groom with them, they cannot fast. ²⁰ But the time will come when the groom is taken away from them, and then they will fast in that day. ²¹ No one sews a patch of unshrunk cloth on an old garment. Otherwise, the new patch pulls away from the old cloth, and a worse tear is made. ²² And no one puts new wine into old wineskins. Otherwise, the wine will burst the skins, and the wine is lost as well as the skins. But new wine is for fresh wineskins."

LORD OF THE SABBATH

²³ On the Sabbath He was going through the grainfields, and His disciples began to make their way picking some heads of grain. ²⁴ The Pharisees said to Him, "Look, why are they doing what is not lawful on the Sabbath?"

²⁵ And He said to them, "Have you never read what David did when he was in need and hungry, he and his companions: ²⁶ how he entered the house of God in the time of Abiathar the high priest and ate the sacred bread—which is not lawful for anyone to eat except the priests—and also gave some to his companions?" ²⁷ Then He told them, "The Sabbath was made for man, and not man for the Sabbath. ²⁸ Therefore the Son of Man is Lord even of the Sabbath."

One man was there who had been sick for thirty-eight years. When Jesus saw him lying there and knew he had already been there a long time, He said to him, "Do you want to get well?"

The Convenience of Sickness
JOHN 5:5-6

One of the most important questions a physician must ask the sick—particularly the long-term sick—is, "Do you want to get well?"

Sick is safe. *Well* is responsible. *Sick* gathers people about us to wait on us and sympathize with our suffering. *Well* gets no such attention. *Sick* is justified leisure. *Well* must shoulder its own vocation. *Sick* may whine and whimper. *Well* must smile and be ignored. So Jesus looked at the man who was sick and asked, "Do you want to get well?"

Does this question make Jesus seem insensitive? "Well, of all the nerve!" the man might have answered, "How dare you suggest that I enjoy my sickness!"

Yet here was a man who for thirty-eight years had been enjoying the power that his sickness gave him over all those around him. For thirty-eight years, or some portion of it, he had some friends to carry him to the pool. He never said out loud that he enjoyed wielding this power over them. Yet if he were healed, he would not be able ever again to order them around. What about all those people in his home who had fetched this or that for him, helped him dress, and cooked his meals just the way he liked them? Once healed, he would lose his power over all these people as well.

Most of all, his self-pity would be gone. When he complained, he would get a lot less sympathy. Nobody would ask him how he became paralyzed in the first place.

So Jesus' question was quite fair: "Do you really want to be well?" The paralytic mulled the question in his mind. Jesus was before him. The poor man must make up his mind. "Do I want to be well? Yes. Yes I do."

"Get up," Jesus told him, "pick up your bedroll and walk!" And he did. Now he was up and walking along the road. Now he carried his own sleeping pallet. He was well. And you know what? It felt good.

What is the next step of faith you need to take? Be careful. It may feel wonderful, but it could involve some heavy requirements.

PRAYER
Lord, there's something harmonious about discord that makes us want to say, "Woe is us!" Cleanse that cheerless spirit from our lives. Make us love the obligations of ministry that come to those who are willing to adopt a positive spirit.

CHAPTER FIVE

THE THIRD SIGN:
HEALING THE SICK

After this a Jewish festival took place, and Jesus went up to Jerusalem. ² By the Sheep Gate in Jerusalem there is a pool, called Bethesda in Hebrew, which has five colonnades. ³ Within these lay a multitude of the sick—blind, lame, and paralyzed—(waiting for the moving of the water, ⁴ because an angel would go down into the pool from time to time and stir up the water. Then the first one who got in after the water was stirred up recovered from whatever ailment he had.)

⁵ One man was there who had been sick for thirty-eight years. ⁶ When Jesus saw him lying there and knew he had already been there a long time, He said to him, "Do you want to get well?"

⁷ "Sir," the sick man answered, "I don't have a man to put me into the pool when the water is stirred up, but while I'm coming, someone goes down ahead of me."

[8] "Get up," Jesus told him, "pick up your bedroll and walk!" [9] Instantly the man got well, picked up his bedroll, and started to walk.

Now that day was the Sabbath, [10] so the Jews said to the man who had been healed, "This is the Sabbath! It's illegal for you to pick up your bedroll."

[11] He replied, "The man who made me well told me, 'Pick up your bedroll and walk.'"

[12] "Who is this man who told you, 'Pick up your bedroll and walk?'" they asked. [13] But the man who was cured did not know who it was, because Jesus had slipped away into the crowd that was there.

[14] After this Jesus found him in the temple complex and said to him, "See, you are well. Do not sin any more, so that something worse doesn't happen to you." [15] The man went and reported to the Jews that it was Jesus who had made him well.

HONORING THE FATHER AND THE SON

[16] Therefore, the Jews began persecuting Jesus because He was doing these things on the Sabbath. [17] But Jesus responded to them, "My Father is still working, and I also am working." [18] This is why the Jews began trying all the more to kill Him: not only was He breaking the Sabbath, but He was even calling God His own Father, making Himself equal with God.

[19] Then Jesus replied, "I assure you: The Son is not able to do anything on His own, but only what He sees the Father doing. For whatever the Father does, these things the Son also does in the same

way. ²⁰ For the Father loves the Son and shows Him everything He is doing, and He will show Him greater works than these so that you will be amazed. ²¹ And just as the Father raises the dead and gives them life, so also the Son gives life to whomever He wishes. ²² The Father, in fact, judges no one but has given all judgment to the Son, ²³ so that all people will honor the Son just as they honor the Father. Anyone who does not honor the Son does not honor the Father who sent Him.

LIFE AND JUDGMENT

²⁴ "I assure you: Anyone who hears My word and believes Him who sent Me has eternal life and will not come under judgment, but has passed from death to life.

²⁵ "I assure you: An hour is coming, and is now here, when the dead will hear the voice of the Son of God, and those who hear will live. ²⁶ For just as the Father has life in Himself, so also He has granted to the Son to have life in Himself. ²⁷ And He has granted Him the right to pass judgment, because He is the Son of Man. ²⁸ Do not be amazed at this, because a time is coming when all who are in the graves will hear His voice ²⁹ and come out—those who have done good things, to the resurrection of life, but those who have done wicked things, to the resurrection of judgment.

³⁰ "I can do nothing on My own. Only as I hear do I judge, and My judgment is righteous, because I do not seek My own will, but the will of Him who sent Me.

FOUR WITNESSES TO JESUS

[31] "If I testify about Myself, My testimony is not valid. [32] There is Another who testifies about Me, and I know that the testimony He gives about Me is valid. [33] You people have sent messengers to John, and he has testified to the truth. [34] I don't receive man's testimony, but I say these things so that you may be saved. [35] John was a burning and shining lamp, and for an hour you were willing to enjoy his light.

[36] "But I have a greater testimony than John's because of the works that the Father has given Me to accomplish. These very works I am doing testify about Me that the Father has sent Me. [37] The Father who sent Me has Himself testified about Me. You have not heard His voice at any time, and you haven't seen His form. [38] You don't have His word living in you, because you don't believe the One He sent. [39] You pore over the Scriptures because you think you have eternal life in them, yet they testify about Me. [40] And you are not willing to come to Me that you may have life.

[41] "I do not accept glory from men, [42] but I know you—that you have no love for God within you. [43] I have come in My Father's name, yet you don't accept Me. If someone else comes in his own name, you will accept him. [44] How can you believe? While accepting glory from one another, you don't seek the glory that comes from the only God. [45] Do not think that I will accuse you to the Father. Your accuser is Moses, on whom you have set your hope. [46] For if you believed Moses, you would believe Me, because he wrote about Me. [47] But if you don't believe his writings, how will you believe My words?"

The Holy Family in the Carpenter Shop

Our blue-collar Savior learned his trade from his blue-collar father. When God became a man he became a tradesman. He who made all things came as a maker of things. The saw and the mallet were his friends. Wood, like life itself, must be cut and shaped to serve. So here is the Holy Family dealing with wood, consecrating themselves to the ordinary glory of plank and saw.

The carpenter-father teaches his carpenter-son to deal with wood.

Across the coming years the sawdust piles up between the two of them. The boy will lengthen in frame until he is man enough to be a man for all seasons. Then he at last gives up the adze and mattock. He abandons the cross-cut and mallet. Then he understands. Wood is why he came. Then at last he deals with wood to lose the moment. Then he leaves the wood to gain eternity. Crosses and redemption are nothing more than the final carpentry of God.

Van Honthorst (1590-1656) was best known for happy genre scenes of common human interaction. In this depiction of a quite ordinary event from the life of Christ, he emphasizes Jesus' humanity, yet also suggests His divinity as the light of the world.

Blessed are the gentle, because they will inherit the earth.

The Happy Gentle

M A T T H E W 5 : 5

The gentle. We are never afraid of gentle people. They are always approachable. They never want to make us afraid. So they become the very arms of God to welcome people into faith.

Here is the great commandment of Christ to those of us in his church. *I command you to be gentle*, to be always approachable. See gentility as an art. It is like a sculpture never finished. Your will to have power will always be set against your desire to be gentle. Others may shun the way of softness and sincerity, choosing instead to make people afraid of them, for those who fear them are more easily controlled. But you must choose to walk a higher—yes, even, a stronger path—the path of gentleness.

Immediately the question arises, If I develop the art of gentility, will people not hurt me? Will I not end up being afraid of them? Would it not be better to intimidate them than to live as one intimidated? No command anywhere in the ethics of the new kingdom tells us we are to out-intimidate the world. Rather, we are to out-gentle it.

Look at the reward Jesus promises to the gentle: They will inherit the earth. "Every athlete who competes exercises self-control in all things," said the apostle Paul. "They do it to receive a perishable crown, but we an imperishable one." (1 Co 9:25).

What is the deportment, then, of those who receive the imperishable crown? Will they wear it proudly as they swagger to the top of the celestial power structure? Hardly. They will likely fall down before "the one seated on the throne, the One who lives forever and ever, the twenty-four elders fall down before the One seated on the throne, worship the One who lives forever and ever, cast their crowns before the throne, and say:

"Our Lord and God,

You are worthy to receive glory and honor and power,

because You have created all things,

and because of Your will they exist and were created" (Rv 4:10,11).

They will lay their crowns at Jesus' feet, because they never intended to rule anyway. What need do they have for crowns? They are simply grateful for their unfading inheritance.

Seek therefore to cultivate gentility. You will not only inherit the earth. You will be like Jesus.

P R A Y E R

Lord, have I ever spoken too loudly to those afraid of me to make them even more fearful? Have I bullied those who reached cautiously and fearfully toward me in hope? Oh Lord, forgive me. Make me gentle, so gentle that those who need you will be unafraid to seek you by reaching to me.

CHAPTER SIX

THE SERMON ON THE MOUNT

When He saw the crowds, He went up on the mountain, and after He sat down, His disciples came to Him. ² Then He began to teach them, saying:

THE BEATITUDES

³ "Blessed are the poor in spirit,
because the kingdom of heaven is
theirs.
⁴ Blessed are those who mourn,
because they will be comforted.
⁵ Blessed are the gentle,
because they will inherit the earth.
⁶ Blessed are those who hunger and
thirst for righteousness,
because they will be filled.
⁷ Blessed are the merciful,
because they will be shown mercy.
⁸ Blessed are the pure in heart,

because they will see God.

9 Blessed are the peacemakers,

because they will be called sons of God.

10 Blessed are those who are persecuted for righteousness,

because the kingdom of heaven is theirs.

11 "Blessed are you when they insult you and persecute you, and say every kind of evil against you falsely because of Me. 12 Be glad and rejoice, because your reward is great in heaven. For that is how they persecuted the prophets who were before you.

BELIEVERS ARE SALT AND LIGHT

13 "You are the salt of the earth. But if the salt should lose its taste, how can it be made salty? It's no longer good for anything but to be thrown out and trampled on by men.

14 "You are the light of the world. A city situated on a hill cannot be hidden. 15 No one lights a lamp and puts it under a basket, but rather on a lampstand, and it gives light for all who are in the house. 16 In the same way, let your light shine before men, so that they may see your good works and give glory to your Father in heaven.

CHRIST FULFILLS THE LAW

17 "Don't assume that I came to destroy the Law or the Prophets. I did not come to destroy but to fulfill. 18 For I assure you: Until heaven and earth pass away, not the smallest letter or one stroke of a letter will ever pass from the law until all things are

accomplished. [19] Therefore, whoever breaks one of the least of these commandments and teaches people to do so, will be called least in the kingdom of heaven. But whoever practices and teaches these commandments, will be called great in the kingdom of heaven. [20] For I tell you, unless your righteousness surpasses that of the scribes and Pharisees, you will never enter the kingdom of heaven.

MURDER BEGINS IN THE HEART

[21] "You have heard that it was said to our ancestors, 'You shall not murder,' and 'whoever murders will be subject to judgment.' [22] But I tell you, everyone who is angry with his brother will be subject to judgment. And whoever says to his brother, 'Fool!' will be subject to the council. But whoever says, 'You moron!' will be subject to hellfire. [23] So if you are offering your gift on the altar, and there you remember that your brother has something against you, [24] leave your gift there in front of the altar. First go and be reconciled with your brother, and then come and offer your gift. [25] Reach a settlement quickly with your adversary, while you're on the way with him, or your adversary will hand you over to the judge, the judge to the officer, and you will be thrown into prison. [26] I assure you: You will never get out of there until you have paid the last penny!

ADULTERY IN THE HEART

[27] "You have heard that it was said, 'You shall not commit adultery.' [28] But I tell you, everyone who looks at a woman to lust for her has already committed adultery with her in his heart. [29] If

your right eye causes you to sin, gouge it out and throw it away. For it is better that you lose one of your members than for your whole body to be thrown into hell. [30] And if your right hand causes you to sin, cut it off and throw it away. For it is better that you lose one of your members than for your whole body to go into hell!

DIVORCE PRACTICES CENSURED

[31] "It was also said, 'Whoever divorces his wife must give her a written notice of divorce.' [32] But I tell you, everyone who divorces his wife, except in a case of sexual immorality, causes her to commit adultery. And whoever marries a divorced woman commits adultery.

TELL THE TRUTH

[33] "Again, you have heard that it was said to our ancestors, 'You must not break your oath, but you must keep your oaths to the Lord.' [34] But I tell you, don't take an oath at all: either by heaven, because it is God's throne; [35] or by the earth, because it is His footstool; or by Jerusalem, because it is the city of the great King. [36] Neither should you swear by your head, because you cannot make a single hair white or black. [37] But let your word 'yes,' be 'yes,' and your 'no,' be 'no.' Anything more than this is from the evil one.

GO THE SECOND MILE

[38] "You have heard that it was said, 'An eye for an eye' and 'a tooth for a tooth.' [39] But I tell you, don't resist an evildoer. On the contrary, if anyone slaps you on your right cheek, turn the other to him also. [40] As for the one who wants to sue you and take away your shirt, let him have your coat as well. [41] And if anyone forces you to

go one mile, go with him two. [42] Give to the one who asks you, and don't turn away from the one who wants to borrow from you.

LOVE YOUR ENEMIES

[43] "You have heard that it was said, 'You shall love your neighbor and hate your enemy.' [44] But I tell you, love your enemies, and pray for those who persecute you, [45] so that you may be sons of your Father in heaven. For He causes His sun to rise on the evil and the good, and sends rain on the righteous and the unrighteous. [46] For if you love those who love you, what reward will you have? Don't even the tax collectors do the same? [47] And if you greet only your brothers, what are you doing out of the ordinary? Don't even the Gentiles do the same? [48] Be perfect, therefore, as your heavenly Father is perfect.

Then He came up and touched the open coffin, and the pallbearers stopped. And He said, "Young man, I tell you, get up!" The dead man sat up and began to speak, and Jesus gave him to his mother.

The Life Giver

LUKE 7:14-15

This woman from Nain had wept twice. She had lost her husband first. Now she had lost her only son. Can desolation know any further atrocity than that she should weep at two funerals?

Now Jesus was here. What would he do? First, he said to the grieving widow, "Don't cry!" Then he came up to the coffin, and the pallbearers came to a halt. He spoke to the dead man! "Young man, I tell you, get up!" The dead man had no choice. Christ had spoken. The man must quit being dead. Thus he sat up and began to speak.

Fear gripped all the people. This kind of eerie miracle seemed almost macabre. It made the skin crawl, the nerves prickle, the hair stand on the back of the neck. Everyone seemed to live in this forbidden zone of surreal silence and stillness—a sea of wide eyes, open mouths, weak knees, and hard swallows.

All except the young man. He spoke while all of the rest of them, somewhere in the valley between elation and horror, stood too dumbfounded to say anything.

What did the young man say? Who can know? Maybe he said, "Hello, Mommy, whose funeral?" Maybe he fairly shouted, "Hallelujah! I have come from the presence of the Almighty to dwell again in the land of the living!" Perhaps he philosophically said, "I'm back. See, death's not as final as we always thought it to be."

Whatever he said, the crowd viewed the miracle with an intermingling of fascination and awe at the all-powerful. The freeze frame erupted into a madhouse. Stony hands began to clap and cheer. Disbelief rained into rejoicing. "Fear came over everyone, and they glorified God, saying, 'A great prophet has risen among us,' and 'God has visited His people.' "

So exists the power of the God we serve, to whom death is but a ranting child—and life an undisputed champion. Jesus cries with those who weep, always touching sorrow with resurrection, either in Nain or in eternity. It is a fearful and wondrous thing to be touched by the living Christ.

PRAYER

Lord, you make demands of death. It whimpers and becomes less a monster than we had thought it to be. How much I need to remember, in moments of grief, what once you did in Nain.

CHAPTER SEVEN

A CENTURION'S FAITH

When He had concluded all His sayings in the hearing of the people, He entered Capernaum. ² A centurion's slave, who was highly valued by him, was sick and about to die. ³ Having heard about Jesus, he sent some Jewish elders to Him, requesting Him to come and save his slave's life. ⁴ When they reached Jesus, they pleaded with Him earnestly, saying, "He is worthy for You to grant this, ⁵ because he loves our nation, and has built us a synagogue." ⁶ Jesus went with them, and when He was not far from the house, the centurion sent friends to tell Him, "Lord, don't trouble Yourself, since I am not worthy to have You come under my roof. ⁷ That is why I didn't even consider myself worthy to come to You. But say the word, and my servant will be cured. ⁸ For I too am a man placed under authority, having soldiers under my command. I say to this one, 'Go!' and he goes; and to another, 'Come!' and he comes; and to my slave, 'Do this!' and he does it."

⁹ Hearing this, Jesus was amazed at him, and turning to the crowd following Him, said, "I tell you, I have

not found so great a faith even in Israel!" [10] When those who had been sent returned to the house, they found the slave in good health.

A WIDOW'S SON RAISED TO LIFE

[11] Soon afterward He was on His way to a town called Nain. His disciples and a large crowd were traveling with Him. [12] Just as He neared the gate of the town, a dead man was being carried out. He was his mother's only son, and she was a widow. A large crowd from the city was also with her. [13] When the Lord saw her, He had compassion on her and said, "Don't cry." [14] Then He came up and touched the open coffin, and the pallbearers stopped. And He said, "Young man, I tell you, get up!"

[15] The dead man sat up and began to speak, and Jesus gave him to his mother. [16] Then fear came over everyone, and they glorified God, saying, "A great prophet has risen among us," and "God has visited His people." [17] This report about Him went throughout Judea and all the vicinity.

IN PRAISE OF JOHN THE BAPTIST

[18] Then John's disciples told him about all these things. So John summoned two of his disciples [19] and sent them to the Lord, asking, "Are You the Coming One, or should we look for someone else?"

[20] When the men reached Him, they said, "John the Baptist sent us to ask You, 'Are You the Coming One, or should we look for someone else?' "

[21] At that time Jesus healed many people of diseases, plagues, and evil spirits, and He granted sight to many blind people. [22] He

replied to them, "Go and report to John the things you have seen and heard: The blind receive their sight, the lame walk, lepers are cleansed, the deaf hear, the dead are raised, and the poor have the good news preached to them. ²³ And blessed is anyone who is not offended because of Me." ²⁴ After John's messengers left, He began to speak to the crowds about John: "What did you go out into the wilderness to see? A reed swaying in the wind? ²⁵ But what did you go out to see? A man dressed in soft robes? Look, those who are splendidly dressed and live in luxury are in royal palaces. ²⁶ But what did you go out to see? A prophet? Yes, I tell you, and far more than a prophet. ²⁷ This is the one of whom it is written:

'Look, I am sending My messenger ahead of You;
He will prepare Your way before You.'

²⁸ I tell you, among those born of women no one is greater than John, but the least in the kingdom of God is greater than he."

²⁹ (And when all the people, including the tax collectors, heard this, they acknowledged God's way of righteousness, because they had been baptized with John's baptism. ³⁰ But since the Pharisees and experts in the law had not been baptized by him, they rejected the plan of God for themselves.)

AN UNRESPONSIVE GENERATION

³¹ "To what then should I compare the people of this generation, and what are they like? ³² They are like children sitting in the marketplace and calling to each other:

'We played the flute for you,
But you didn't dance;

We sang a lament,

But you didn't weep!'

[33] For John the Baptist did not come eating bread or drinking wine, and you say, 'He has a demon!' [34] The Son of Man has come eating and drinking, and you say, 'Look, a glutton and a drunkard, a friend of tax collectors and sinners!' [35] Yet wisdom is vindicated by all her children."

MUCH FORGIVENESS, MUCH LOVE

[36] Then one of the Pharisees invited Him to eat with him. He entered the Pharisee's house and reclined at the table. [37] And a woman in the town who was a sinner found out that Jesus was reclining at the table in the Pharisee's house. She brought an alabaster flask of fragrant oil [38] and stood behind Him at His feet, weeping, and began to wash His feet with her tears. She wiped His feet with the hair of her head, kissing them and anointing them with the fragrant oil.

[39] When the Pharisee who had invited Him saw this, he said to himself, "This man, if He were a prophet, would know who and what kind of woman this is who is touching Him—that she's a sinner!"

[40] Jesus replied to him, "Simon, I have something to say to you."

"Teacher," he said, "say it."

[41] "A creditor had two debtors. One owed five hundred denarii, and the other fifty. [42] Since they could not pay it back, he graciously forgave them both. So, which of them will love him more?"

[43] Simon answered, "I suppose the one he forgave more."

"You have judged correctly," He told him. [44] Turning to the woman, He said to Simon, "Do you see this woman? I entered your house; you gave Me no water for My feet, but she, with her tears, has washed My feet and wiped them with her hair. [45] You gave Me no kiss, but she hasn't stopped kissing My feet since I came in. [46] You didn't anoint My head with oil, but she has anointed My feet with fragrant oil. [47] Therefore I tell you, her many sins have been forgiven; that's why she loved much. But the one who is forgiven little, loves little." [48] Then He said to her, "Your sins are forgiven."

[49] Those who were at the table with Him began to say among themselves, "Who is this man who even forgives sins?"

[50] And He said to the woman, "Your faith has saved you. Go in peace."

Then the disciples came up and asked Him, "Why do You speak to them in parables?". . . "For this reason I speak to them in parables, because looking they do not see, and hearing they do not listen or understand."

When Heaven Told Stories
MATTHEW 13:10,13

Stories are the life's blood of truth. Without stories, the heart of relationship is gone. Insight alone may lull the mind to sleep. But prick a sleepy, disinterested audience with a story, and intrigue wakes the heart and locks the truth inside. Story dresses truth in the garments of intrigue.

Jesus chose to teach in stories. In parables. Why? Because stories are expositional. Pity all those purely precept preachers who believe that stories do not carry biblical exposition. So often when Jesus was asked some question relating to the law, he got expository. When asked, "Who is my neighbor?" he answered with the story of the Good Samaritan. When Pharisees criticized him for eating with the spiritually lost, he told three stories (see Luke 15, page 117). When a fellow diner told him all who ate at the final banquet of God would be blessed, he told the parable of the great banquet. When his disciples asked him to teach them to pray, he gave them the Lord's Prayer and then told them the story of the persistent widow.

Stories were Jesus' approach to teaching. He told them everywhere. Jesus always emphasized the mystical meaning of his stories. Every child in Sunday school knows the definition of parable as an "earthly story with a heavenly meaning." The definition is not too far off. Jesus said that parables would be stories which the believers would understand but unbelievers would not. Sometimes the mystery that attended his stories, however, was cloaked even to his disciples. Even the disciples did not fully understand the parable of the sower and the seed, and Jesus had to explain it to them. What mortal minds could never understand in theory, they could at least approach in prose.

Jesus was the supreme storyteller. His stories have marked history. The stories, powerfully narrated, answered Jesus' critics and instructed his church. The kingdom of God was born between the grand "once upon a time" of Bethlehem and the "happy ever after" of the Resurrection. Jesus' stories packaged the timeless doctrines of Christianity. Now your story and mine live out those doctrines every day.

PRAYER
Lord, we remind ourselves that the method of the kingdom is one grand story composed of many smaller ones. Stories fascinate us. Stories instruct us. Your story is called the gospel. Our story is called our personal testimony. Between your story and ours lies all the meaning available in this world.

CHAPTER EIGHT

FROM THE GOSPEL OF MATTHEW, CHAPTER 13

THE PARABLE OF THE SOWER

O n that day Jesus went out of the house and was sitting by the sea. ² Such large crowds gathered around Him that He got into a boat and sat down, while the whole crowd stood on the shore.

³ Then He told them many things in parables, saying: "Consider the sower who went out to sow. ⁴ As he was sowing, some seeds fell along the path, and the birds came and ate them up. ⁵ Others fell on rocky ground, where they didn't have much soil, and they sprang up quickly since they had no deep soil. ⁶ But when the sun came up they were scorched, and since they had no root, they withered. ⁷ Others fell among thorns, and the thorns came up and choked them. ⁸ Still others fell on good ground, and produced a crop: some a hundred, some sixty, and some thirty times what was sown. ⁹ Anyone who has ears should listen!"

WHY JESUS USED PARABLES

¹⁰ Then the disciples came up and asked Him, "Why do You speak to them in parables?"

[11] He answered them, "To know the secrets of the kingdom of heaven has been granted to you, but to them it has not been granted. [12] For whoever has, more will be given to him, and he will have more than enough. But whoever does not have, even what he has will be taken away from him. [13] For this reason I speak to them in parables, because looking they do not see, and hearing they do not listen or understand. [14] In them the prophecy of Isaiah is fulfilled that says:

> 'You will listen and listen,
> yet never understand;
> and you will look and look,
> yet never perceive.
> [15] For this people's heart has grown callous;
> their ears are hard of hearing
> and they have shut their eyes;
> otherwise they might see with their eyes
> and hear with their ears,
> understand with their hearts
> and turn back—and I would cure them.'

[16] "But your eyes are blessed because they do see, and your ears because they do hear! [17] For I assure you: Many prophets and righteous people longed to see the things you see, yet didn't see them; to hear the things you hear, yet didn't hear them.

THE PARABLE OF
THE SOWER EXPLAINED

18 "You, then, listen to the parable of the sower: 19 When anyone hears the word about the kingdom and doesn't understand it, the evil one comes and snatches away what was sown in his heart. This is the one sown along the path. 20 And the one sown on rocky ground—this is one who hears the word and immediately receives it with joy. 21 Yet he has no root in himself, but is short-lived. When pressure or persecution comes because of the word, immediately he stumbles. 22 Now the one sown among the thorns—this is one who hears the word, but the worries of this age and the pleasure of wealth choke the word, and it becomes unfruitful. 23 But the one sown on the good ground—this is one who hears and understands the word, who does bear fruit and produce: some a hundred, some sixty, some thirty times what was sown."

THE PARABLE OF
THE WHEAT AND THE WEEDS

24 He presented another parable to them: "The kingdom of heaven may be compared to a man who sowed good seed in his field. 25 But while people were sleeping, his enemy came, sowed weeds among the wheat, and left. 26 When the plants sprouted and produced grain, then the weeds also appeared. 27 The landowner's slaves came to him and said, 'Master, didn't you sow good seed in your field? Then where did the weeds come from?'

28 " 'An enemy did this!' he told them.

" 'So, do you want us to go and gather them up?' the slaves asked him.

²⁹ " 'No,' he said. 'When you gather up the weeds, you might also uproot the wheat with them. ³⁰ Let both grow together until the harvest. At harvest time I'll tell the reapers, "Gather the weeds first and tie them in bundles to burn them, but store the wheat in my barn.' "

THE PARABLES OF THE MUSTARD SEED AND OF THE YEAST

³¹ He presented another parable to them: "The kingdom of heaven is like a mustard seed that a man took and sowed in his field. ³² It's the smallest of all the seeds, but when grown, it's taller than the vegetables and becomes a tree, so that the birds of the sky come and nest in its branches."

³³ He told them another parable: "The kingdom of heaven is like yeast that a woman took and mixed into three measures of flour until it spread through all of it."

USING PARABLES FULFILLS PROPHECY

³⁴ Jesus told the crowds all these things in parables, and He would not speak anything to them without a parable, ³⁵ so that what was spoken through the prophet might be fulfilled:

> "I will open My mouth in parables;
> I will declare things kept secret from the foundation of the world."

JESUS INTERPRETS THE WHEAT AND THE WEEDS

36 Then He dismissed the crowds and went into the house. And His disciples approached Him and said, "Explain the parable of the weeds in the field to us."

37 He replied: "The One who sows the good seed is the Son of Man; 38 the field is the world; and the good seed—these are the sons of the kingdom. The weeds are the sons of the evil one, and 39 the enemy who sowed them is the Devil. The harvest is the end of the age, and the harvesters are angels. 40 Therefore just as the weeds are gathered and burned in the fire, so it will be at the end of the age. 41 The Son of Man will send out His angels, and they will gather from His kingdom everything that causes sin and those guilty of lawlessness. 42 They will throw them into the blazing furnace where there will be weeping and gnashing of teeth. 43 Then the righteous will shine like the sun in their Father's kingdom. Anyone who has ears should listen!

THE PARABLES OF THE HIDDEN TREASURE AND OF THE PRICELESS PEARL

44 "The kingdom of heaven is like treasure, buried in a field, that a man found and reburied. Then in his joy he goes and sells everything he has and buys that field.

45 "Again, the kingdom of heaven is like a merchant in search of fine pearls. 46 When he found one priceless pearl, he went and sold everything he had, and bought it.

THE PARABLE OF THE NET

[47] "Again, the kingdom of heaven is like a large net thrown into the sea. It collected every kind of fish, [48] and when it was full, they dragged it ashore, sat down, and gathered the good fish into containers, but threw out the worthless ones. [49] So it will be at the end of the age. The angels will go out, separate the evil who are among the righteous, [50] and throw them into the blazing furnace. In that place there will be weeping and gnashing of teeth.

THE STOREHOUSE OF TRUTH

[51] "Have you understood all these things?"

"Yes," they told Him.

[52] "Therefore," He said to them, "every student of Scripture instructed in the kingdom of heaven is like a landowner who brings out of his storeroom what is new and what is old." [53] When Jesus had finished these parables, He left there.

REJECTION AT NAZARETH

[54] Having come to His hometown, He began to teach them in their synagogue, so that they were astonished and said, "How did this wisdom and these miracles come to Him? [55] Isn't this the carpenter's son? Isn't His mother called Mary, and His brothers James, Joseph, Simon, and Judas? [56] And His sisters, aren't they all with us? So where does He get all these things?" [57] And they were offended by Him.

But Jesus said to them, "A prophet is not without honor except in his hometown and in his household." [58] And He did not do many miracles there because of their unbelief.

The Sermon on the Mount

There precedes the Christian church a preacher and a sermon. Jesus is the preacher, whose sermons were not only riveting but insightful. See these truths that spell out in Aramaic verbs and nouns, wisdom running through time in an alphabet of grace. Look at how this sermon changes all who attend it. The blessings spill out upon the poor of spirit. The meek and the gentle see themselves as worthy. The selfish repent of their greed. The proud bow their heads. The needy are satisfied.

The Sermon on the Mount is to the New Testament as the Ten Commandments are in the Old. This small sermon can be preached in eighteen minutes, yet it contains all that the church believes about the Ten Commandments and the motives which precede them. Herein lie the teachings on ethics, prayer, family, discipleship, and the kingdom of God.

Let every sermon hastily prepared and poorly delivered ask itself to learn the mighty form of words carefully and mightily crafted to change the world.

Lorrain (1600-1682) became famous for his idyllic landscapes, avoiding harsh lighting by painting morning or late afternoon scenes. Here he emphasizes the centrality of Christ, not by dramatic effect, but with the royal blue of Jesus' cloak against a golden aura.

Aren't two sparrows sold for a penny? Yet not one of them falls to the ground without your Father's consent. But even the hairs of your head have all been counted. Don't be afraid therefore; you are worth more than many sparrows.

The Soul's True Worth
MATTHEW 10:29-31

Visualize the vault of God! In this vault he keeps the precious things of eternity. In his vault are all those people who mean so much to him. In this file is your person-hood. There are your fingerprints—unique in every way! There is a list of pertinent statistics—when you were born, when you will die, a list of your strengths, a list of your charitable acts. There also is listed the number of hairs on your head.

Across the front of this file God has stamped the word *mine*. Under the word *mine* is the signature of God. Jesus said that God, meticulous in keeping track of his world, has numbered the sparrows. Therefore, we are to rejoice, for we are worth more than many sparrows.

In the face of all we mean to God, why do we so often mean so little to ourselves? Low self-esteem afflicts almost everyone at one time or another. Whenever we suffer from it, should we not stop and ask ourselves, Have we any right to feel badly about something that God feels so good about? Probably not! To be loved with such over-whelming love as God sheds upon us makes our not loving ourselves a strong dis-agreement with God. When we disagree with God, are we not acting as though God has made a mistake?

Is there evidence that we are wrong in not loving ourselves and that God is right in not agreeing with us? Of course there is.

There stands the cross of Christ! Here is the opinion of God: "I love you. If you do not love yourself, you fail to understand the day my only begotten Son died there on Calvary. In Gethsemane, the night before his cross, he would have chosen another evidence that he might honor the fact that I was in love with you. There was no other way. Study the dying of my Son. Can you still feel worthless? Consider what you are worth to me. His hands bear the mark of that great expense my son and I both paid. Aren't two sparrows sold for a penny? You are worth more than many sparrows."

PRAYER
Lord, I can see I am worth much more than I sometimes feel I am. You have loved me so much, how dare I disagree with you.

CHAPTER NINE

COMMISSIONING THE TWELVE

S ummoning His twelve disciples, He gave them authority over unclean spirits, to drive them out, and to heal every disease and every sickness. ² These are the names of the twelve apostles:

> First, Simon, who is called Peter, and
> Andrew his brother;
> James the son of Zebedee, and John
> his brother;
> ³ Philip and Bartholomew;
> Thomas and Matthew the tax collector;
> James the son of Alphaeus, and
> Thaddaeus;
> ⁴ Simon the Zealot, and Judas Iscariot,
> who also betrayed Him.

⁵ Jesus sent out these twelve after giving them instructions: "Don't take the road leading to other nations, and don't enter any Samaritan town. ⁶ Instead, go to the lost sheep of the house of Israel. ⁷ As you go,

announce this: 'The kingdom of heaven has come near.' [8] Heal the sick, raise the dead, cleanse the lepers, drive out demons. You have received free of charge; give free of charge. [9] Don't take along gold, silver, or copper for your money-belts, [10] or a backpack for the road, or an extra shirt, or sandals, or a walking stick, for the worker is worthy of his food.

[11] "Whatever town or village you enter, find out who is worthy, and stay there until you leave. [12] Greet a household when you enter it, [13] and if the household is worthy, your peace should come upon it. But if it is unworthy, your peace should return to you. [14] If anyone will not welcome you or listen to your words, shake the dust off your feet when you leave that house or town. [15] I assure you: It will be more tolerable on the day of judgment for the land of Sodom and Gomorrah than for that town.

PERSECUTIONS PREDICTED

[16] "Look, I'm sending you out like sheep among wolves. Therefore be as shrewd as serpents and harmless as doves. [17] Because people will hand you over to sanhedrins and flog you in their synagogues, beware of them. [18] You will even be brought before governors and kings because of Me, to bear witness to them and to the nations. [19] But when they hand you over, don't worry about how or what you should speak. For you will be given what to say at that hour, [20] because you are not speaking, but the Spirit of your Father is speaking in you.

[21] "Brother will betray brother to death, and a father his child. Children will even rise up against their parents and have them put

to death. 22 You will be hated by everybody because of My name. And the one who endures to the end will be delivered. 23 But when they persecute you in one town, move on to another. For I assure you: You will not have covered the towns of Israel before the Son of Man comes. 24 A disciple is not above his teacher, or a slave above his master. 25 It is enough for a disciple to become like his teacher and a slave like his master. If they called the head of the house 'Beelzebul,' how much more the members of his household.

FEAR GOD

26 "Therefore, don't be afraid of them, since there is nothing covered that won't be uncovered, and nothing hidden that won't be made known. 27 What I tell you in the dark, speak in the light. What you hear in a whisper, proclaim on the housetops. 28 Don't fear those who kill the body but are not able to kill the soul; but rather, fear Him who is able to destroy both soul and body in hell. 29 Aren't two sparrows sold for a penny? Yet not one of them falls to the ground without your Father's consent. 30 But even the hairs of your head have all been counted. 31 Don't be afraid therefore; you are worth more than many sparrows.

ACKNOWLEDGING CHRIST

32 "Therefore, everyone who will acknowledge Me before men, I will also acknowledge Him before My Father in heaven. 33 But whoever denies Me before men, I will also deny him before My Father in heaven. 34 Don't assume that I came to bring peace on

the earth. I did not come to bring peace, but a sword. [35] For I came to turn

> A man against his father,
>
> a daughter against her mother,
>
> a daughter-in-law against her mother-in-law,
>
> [36] and a man's enemies will be the members of his household.

[37] The person who loves father or mother more than Me is not worthy of Me; the person who loves son or daughter more than Me is not worthy of Me. [38] And whoever doesn't take up his cross and follow Me is not worthy of Me. [39] Anyone finding his life will lose it, and anyone losing his life because of Me will find it.

A CUP OF COLD WATER

[40] "The one who welcomes you welcomes Me, and the one who welcomes Me welcomes Him who sent Me. [41] Anyone who welcomes a prophet because he is a prophet will receive a prophet's reward. And anyone who welcomes a righteous person because he's righteous will receive a righteous person's reward. [42] And whoever gives just a cup of cold water to one of these little ones because he is a disciple—I assure you: He will never lose his reward!"

Christ with the Roman Centurion

Dwarfed by the majestic façade of the Fortress Antonia, Jesus and the Romans confronted each other. We, the would-be innocent, behold their confrontation. They represented two kingdoms, and the political kingdom has always appeared to be the dominant one. But as empires have come and gone, the real kingdom remains unchanged—this kingdom is in every generation the community of the cross. New we cry inwardly, for we understand both kingdoms. We have been a part of both; we still are. One sends forth soldiers, the other evangelists. One divides the world into provinces, the other into mission fields. One proclaims the state; the other heralds the gospel of the Word.

Both kingdoms were real, but the Romans could not understand the reality of Jesus' kingdom. What nonsense spoke of "the kingdom of God" within the empire of Caesar? Caesar fought with armor and blade, not with the sermons of a Nazarene carpenter or his disciples.

By Calvin Miller, From *Once upon a Tree*, Baker Book House

Jean Jouvenet (1644-1717) was the leading French religious painter of his generation, known for works that united realism with baroque emotionalism. Here, the centurion gladly sacrifices his symbols of power and prestige before the gentle Christ.

Jesus said to them, "I assure you: Moses didn't give you the bread from heaven, but My Father gives you the true bread from heaven. For the bread of God is the One who comes down from heaven and gives life to the world."

The Manna Eaters

JOHN 6:32-33

The crowd that day reminded Jesus that they were like the ancient Israelites. God had given ancient Israel manna to eat in the desert, in the wilderness. Jesus had just given modern Israel bread to eat. The manna God had given ancient Israel was a miracle—no doubt about it! Somehow, strangely, it had appeared on the ground with the morning dews. Now Jesus had given them bread to eat—bread out of nothing, and a bottomless basket of it. No doubt about that either!

So Jesus gave them a little reminder, a little history lesson, about how temporary that ancient manna was. You couldn't collect tomorrow's manna ahead of time, for it would spoil. This was God's way of reminding Israel that his people were to depend on him one day at a time. Yesterday's manna just wouldn't keep!

But the issue was even bigger than food and full stomachs. Yesterday's miracles wouldn't keep, either. The manna had been miraculous enough to give them biological life and to keep them alive one day at a time. Each morning when they awoke, they had to remember all over again: they were still hungry. They needed more miracle bread today, or they would starve. Finally, they all died. Manna wasn't great enough to give them life eternal.

So Jesus said frankly, "This bread I just gave you, like manna of old, will not keep you alive for long. There is better bread! It is not a loaf to be ingested, but bread to be received into your heart. It will nourish you for eternity. Seek this loaf! Eat and never die! Taste, savor, and be filled forever!"

Yet we always prefer the bread we can toast to the kind that we can't.

So the people would turn away in time, just as millions have waved the hand with a "Thanks, no thanks" throughout the centuries. The bread that would nourish them forever is a hard loaf to market when the sun is shining, when the belly is full, and when the world feels that it's in no immediate danger of dying.

PRAYER

Lord, I get hungry at least three times every day. I still eat a lot of bread. I wonder why I never get as hungry for the bread that nourishes eternally. Forgive my shallow appetites. Teach me a better hunger, a hunger to do your will.

CHAPTER TEN

THE FOURTH SIGN: FEEDING FIVE THOUSAND

After this Jesus crossed the Sea of Galilee (or Tiberias). 2 And a huge crowd was following Him because they saw the signs that He was performing on the sick. 3 So Jesus went up a mountain and sat down there with His disciples.

4 Now the Passover, a Jewish festival, was near. 5 Therefore, when Jesus raised His eyes and noticed a huge crowd coming toward Him, He asked Philip, "Where will we buy bread so these people can eat?" 6 He asked this to test him, for He Himself knew what He was going to do.

7 Philip answered, "Two hundred denarii worth of bread wouldn't be enough for each of them to have a little."

8 One of His disciples, Andrew, Simon Peter's brother, said to Him, 9 "There's a boy here who has five barley loaves and two fish—but what are they for so many?"

¹⁰ Then Jesus said, "Have the people sit down."

There was plenty of grass in that place, so the men sat down, numbering about five thousand. ¹¹ Then Jesus took the loaves, and after giving thanks He distributed them to those who were seated; so also with the fish, as much as they wanted.

¹² When they were full, He told His disciples, "Collect the leftovers so that nothing is wasted." ¹³ So they collected them and filled twelve baskets with the pieces from the five barley loaves that were left over by those who had eaten.

¹⁴ When the people saw the sign He had done, they said, "This really is the Prophet who was to come into the world!" ¹⁵ Therefore, when Jesus knew that they were about to come and take Him by force to make Him king, He withdrew again to the mountain by Himself.

THE FIFTH SIGN:
WALKING ON WATER

¹⁶ When evening came, His disciples went down to the sea, ¹⁷got into a boat, and started across the sea to Capernaum. Darkness had already set in, but Jesus had not yet come to them. ¹⁸ Then a high wind arose, and the sea began to churn. ¹⁹ After they had rowed about three or four miles, they saw Jesus walking on the sea. He was coming near the boat, and they were afraid.

²⁰ But He said to them, "It is I. Don't be afraid!" ²¹ Then they were willing to take Him on board, and at once the boat was at the shore where they were heading.

THE BREAD OF LIFE

²² The next day, the crowd that had stayed on the other side of the sea knew there had been only one boat. They also knew that Jesus had not boarded the boat with His disciples, but His disciples had gone off alone. ²³ Some boats from Tiberias came near the place where they ate the bread after the Lord gave thanks. ²⁴ When the crowd saw that neither Jesus nor His disciples were there, they got into the boats and went to Capernaum, looking for Jesus.

²⁵ When they found Him on the other side of the sea, they said to Him, "Rabbi, when did You get here?"

²⁶ Jesus answered, "I assure you: You are looking for Me, not because you saw the signs, but because you ate the loaves and were filled. ²⁷ Don't work for the food that perishes but for the food that lasts for eternal life, which the Son of Man will give you, because on Him God the Father has set His seal of approval."

²⁸ "What can we do to perform the works of God?" they asked.

²⁹ Jesus replied, "This is the work of God: that you believe in the One He has sent."

³⁰ "Then what sign are You going to do so we may see and believe You?" they asked. "What are You going to perform? ³¹ Our fathers ate the manna in the desert, just as it is written: 'He gave them bread from heaven to eat.' "

³² Jesus said to them, "I assure you: Moses didn't give you the bread from heaven, but My Father gives you the true bread from heaven. ³³ For the bread of God is the One who comes down from heaven and gives life to the world."

³⁴ Then they said, "Sir, give us this bread always!"

³⁵ "I am the bread of life," Jesus told them. "No one who comes to Me will ever be hungry, and no one who believes in Me will ever be thirsty again. ³⁶ But as I told you, you've seen Me, and yet you do not believe. ³⁷ Everyone the Father gives Me will come to Me, and the one who comes to Me I will never cast out. ³⁸ For I have come down from heaven, not to do My will, but the will of Him who sent Me. ³⁹ This is the will of Him who sent Me: that I should lose none of those He has given Me but should raise them up on the last day. ⁴⁰ For this is the will of My Father: that everyone who sees the Son and believes in Him may have eternal life, and I will raise him up on the last day."

⁴¹ Therefore the Jews started complaining about Him, because He said, "I am the bread that came down from heaven." ⁴² They were saying, "Isn't this Jesus the son of Joseph, whose father and mother we know? How can He now say, 'I have come down from heaven'?"

⁴³ Jesus answered them, "Stop complaining among yourselves. ⁴⁴ No one can come to Me unless the Father who sent Me draws him, and I will raise him up on the last day. ⁴⁵ It is written in the Prophets: 'And they will all be taught by God.' Everyone who has listened to and learned from the Father comes to Me— ⁴⁶ not that anyone has seen the Father except the One who is from God. He has seen the Father.

⁴⁷ "I assure you: Anyone who believes has eternal life. ⁴⁸ I am the bread of life. ⁴⁹ Your fathers ate the manna in the desert, and they died. ⁵⁰ This is the bread that comes down from heaven so that

anyone may eat of it and not die. ⁵¹ I am the living bread that came down from heaven. If anyone eats of this bread he will live forever. The bread that I will give for the life of the world is My flesh."

⁵² At that, the Jews argued among themselves, "How can this man give us His flesh to eat?"

⁵³ So Jesus said to them, "I assure you: Unless you eat the flesh of the Son of Man and drink His blood, you do not have life in yourselves. ⁵⁴ Anyone who eats My flesh and drinks My blood has eternal life, and I will raise him up on the last day, ⁵⁵ because My flesh is true food and My blood is true drink. ⁵⁶ The one who eats My flesh and drinks My blood lives in Me, and I in him. ⁵⁷ Just as the living Father sent Me and I live because of the Father, so the one who feeds on Me will live because of Me. ⁵⁸ This is the bread that came down from heaven; it is not like the manna your fathers ate— and they died. The one who eats this bread will live forever."

⁵⁹ He said these things while teaching in the synagogue in Capernaum.

MANY DISCIPLES DESERT JESUS

⁶⁰ Therefore, when many of His disciples heard this, they said, "This teaching is hard! Who can accept it?"

⁶¹ Jesus, knowing in Himself that His disciples were complaining about this, asked them, "Does this offend you? ⁶² Then what if you were to observe the Son of Man ascending to where He was before? ⁶³ The Spirit is the One who gives life. The flesh doesn't help at all. The words that I have spoken to you are spirit and are life. ⁶⁴ But there are some among you who don't believe." (For

Jesus knew from the beginning those who would not believe and the one who would betray Him.) [65] He said, "This is why I told you that no one can come to Me unless it is granted to him by the Father."

[66] From that moment many of His disciples turned back and no longer walked with Him. [67] Therefore Jesus said to the Twelve, "You don't want to go away too, do you?"

[68] Simon Peter answered, "Lord, to whom should we go? You have the words of eternal life. [69] And we have come to believe and know that You are the Holy One of God!"

[70] Jesus replied to them, "Didn't I choose you, the Twelve? Yet one of you is the Devil!" [71] He was referring to Judas, Simon Iscariot's son, one of the Twelve, because he was going to betray Him.

Christ Walking on the Water

GALILEE

Only once was Galilee
   hard-set as concrete.
Only once did her soft liquid
   face turn water into
   granite
Then he who at her long-ago
creation
   said engulfing waves
   should be her nature
Stepped on her sinking
   softness
And Galilee grew rigid
   at the slightest
   touch of royal
   feet.
His sandals
   traced his
   footprints
   on the sea
As she became
   a highway
   for her Lord.

By Calvin Miller,
From *My Journal*

Kupman painted this work in 1910, which captures the storm's violence in Post-Impressionistic and Expressionistic styles. By painting the disciples and the boat between Christ's outstretched arms, he shows Jesus embracing and comforting His followers.

Immediately after hearing about Him, a woman whose little daughter had an unclean spirit came and fell at His feet. Now the woman was Greek, a Syrophoenician by birth, and she kept asking Him to drive the demon out of her daughter.

The Wideness of Mercy

MARK 7:25-26

Jesus probably went to Tyre to get away from the demanding crowds of Galilee. When he got there, he found a poor Gentile woman who needed him badly. Christ's gospel stood the test! How widely will the Good News serve? Already, Jesus had worked with the Samaritan woman and had led half-breed Jews to his Father. Here was a Gentile woman who had never been a Jew, and yet she had a great need.

The woman was a mother. Her motherhood cried out in behalf of her poor daughter. Jesus tried to give her the Jewish answer as to why he would not help. She was a mere Palestinian; he was a Jew. The Jews characteristically took a dim view of those who were not "God's chosen people!"

But Jesus did not believe the gospel was just for Jews. Nor did he intone the old rabbi's prayer, "I thank God I am not a dog, a Gentile, or a woman." Jesus wanted the woman to know how things were between Jews and Gentiles. Hence, he reminded her how Jews generally felt.

Undaunted, the woman's plea continued. It was heart-rending. What was the Messiah to do? She had a need. She had his ear. And she had her faith. So he told her that her daughter was healed.

Human bias and prejudice makes us want to pick and choose the recipients of God's favor. But this Gentile woman saw firsthand how big and transnational God's grace is. This same grace would at last stretch out his arms upon the cross in a world-wide embrace. All who would cry for mercy, whatever their continent or color, would be able to find the embrace of God. Jesus would save to the uttermost all who would call upon him.

You cannot trust Christ and love narrowly, for the love of Christ is blatantly inclusive. Follow Jesus long enough, and sooner or later he's apt to save someone you don't much care for. Then you will have to see if you can learn to love those unlovely people that God seems to love as much as he loves you.

PRAYER

Lord, I am glad that you save to the uttermost all who call upon you. I am a Gentile. You are a Jew. But no matter! The walls are down now. Redemption is as inclusive as the air around us.

CHAPTER ELEVEN

THE TRADITIONS OF THE ELDERS

The Pharisees and some of the scribes who had come from Jerusalem gathered around Him. [2] They observed that some of His disciples were eating their bread with unclean—that is, unwashed—hands. [3] (For the Pharisees, in fact all the Jews, will not eat unless they wash their hands ritually, keeping the tradition of the elders. [4] When they come from the marketplace, they do not eat unless they have washed. And there are many other customs they have received and keep, like the washing of cups, jugs, copper utensils, and dining couches.) [5] Then the Pharisees and the scribes asked Him, "Why don't Your disciples live according to the tradition of the elders, instead of eating bread with ritually unclean hands?"

[6] But He said to them, "Isaiah prophesied correctly about you hypocrites, as it is written:

> 'This people honors Me with their
> lips,

but their heart is far from Me.

⁷ They worship Me in vain,

teaching as doctrines the commands of men.'

⁸ Disregarding the commandment of God, you keep the tradition of men." ⁹ He also said to them, "You splendidly disregard God's commandment, so that you may maintain your tradition! ¹⁰ For Moses said:

'Honor your father and your mother;' and,

'Whoever speaks evil of father or mother must be put to death.'

¹¹ But you say, 'If a man tells his father or mother, "Whatever benefit you might have received from me is *'Corban'*"' (that is, a gift committed to the temple), ¹² you no longer let him do anything for his father or mother. ¹³ You revoke God's word by your tradition that you have handed down. And you do many other similar things." ¹⁴ Summoning the crowd again, He told them, "Listen to Me, all of you, and understand: ¹⁵ Nothing that goes into a man from outside can defile him, but the things that come out of a man are what defile a man. ¹⁶ If anyone has ears to hear, he should listen!"

¹⁷ When He went into the house away from the crowd, the disciples asked Him about the parable. ¹⁸ And He said to them, "Are you also as lacking in understanding? Don't you realize that nothing going into a man from the outside can defile him? ¹⁹ For it doesn't go into his heart but into the stomach, and is eliminated." (As a result, He made all foods clean.) ²⁰ Then He said, "What comes out of a man—that defiles a man. ²¹ For from within, out of people's

hearts, come evil thoughts, sexual immoralities, thefts, murders, [22] adulteries, greed, evil actions, deceit, lewdness, stinginess, blasphemy, pride, and foolishness. [23] All these evil things come from within and defile a man."

A GENTILE MOTHER'S FAITH

[24] From there He got up and departed to the region of Tyre and Sidon. He entered a house and did not want anyone to know it, but He could not escape notice. [25] Instead, immediately after hearing about Him, a woman whose little daughter had an unclean spirit came and fell at His feet. [26] Now the woman was Greek, a Syrophoenician by birth, and she kept asking Him to drive the demon out of her daughter. [27] And He said to her, "Allow the children to be satisfied first, because it isn't right to take the children's bread and throw it to the dogs."

[28] But she replied to Him, "Lord, even the dogs under the table eat the children's crumbs."

[29] Then He told her, "Because of this reply, you may go. The demon has gone out of your daughter." [30] When she went back to her home, she found her child lying on the bed, and the demon was gone.

JESUS DOES EVERYTHING WELL

[31] Again, leaving the region of Tyre, He went by way of Sidon to the Sea of Galilee, through the region of the Decapolis. [32] And they brought to Him a deaf man who also had a speech difficulty, and begged Him to lay His hand on him. [33] So He took him away

from the crowd privately. After putting His fingers in the man's ears and spitting, He touched his tongue. 34 Then, looking up to heaven, He sighed deeply and said to him, "Ephphatha!" (that is, "Be opened!"). 35 Immediately his ears were opened, his speech difficulty was removed, and he began to speak clearly. 36 Then He ordered them to tell no one, but the more He would order them, the more they would proclaim it.

37 They were extremely astonished and said, "He has done everything well! He even makes deaf people hear, and people unable to speak, talk!"

Christ with Mary and Martha

This resentment of waste may have been the very issue behind Thursday's bargain with the priests. Only four days before in nearby Bethany, Mary, the sister of the resurrected Lazarus, had done something that appeared to Judas to be wasteful and extravagant (John 12:1-3). She had taken a pound of spikenard, a costly fragrance, and poured it on Jesus' feet. Spikenard was a rare Himalayan flower, and many thousands of these precious blossoms had to be crushed to produce a pound of the fragrant oil. The ointment was so costly that the price of the one pound that Mary had lavished on Jesus would have kept some poor family in food for a whole year.

The price of the spikenard would have doubtless gone a long way also in supporting an itinerant rabbi and his retinue. Judas explosively condemned the waste: "Why wasn't this fragrant oil sold for three hundred denarii and given to the poor?" (John 12:5). Nevertheless, Jesus defended Mary's deed and spoke with a curt finality that Judas could not possibly mistake: "Leave her alone; she has kept it for the day of My burial." (v. 7).

Taken from *Once Upon A Tree* by Calvin Miller, pp. 94-95

Vermeer (1632-1675) was the most famous of the "Little Dutch Masters," excelling at quiet scenes that showed people engaged in common duties. In characteristic simplicity, he here groups Mary, Martha, and Christ together in a serene moment of community.

"But you," He asked them, "who do you say that I am?" Simon Peter answered, "You are the Messiah, the Son of the living God!"

Thou Art the Christ
MATTHEW 16:15-16

God has one great task for every person: Find out who Jesus is. That completed, you face the second task: Announce the discovery to others.

In our day when we think everyone knows who Jesus is, we easily wonder why Peter's confession seemed to be so inspiring to Christ. The answer, of course, is that Peter's confession came out of his own inner research. It did not, as ours, come from a long-standing historical perspective. Peter had no perspective. Attaining faith for us is like drawing the picture of a house from a hilltop where we can see it all from a distance. Peter was trying to draw the house while walking around its rooms and hallways.

Much of what we know to be true of Christ, we have been able to compute because we have the advantage of looking back over twenty centuries of study and thought. We have the New Testament Scriptures. We have a heritage of saints who have practiced the faith. We have people we know who have lived their entire lives in response to Christ's call. Peter, being there when it happened, had to figure out exactly how to make up his own mind about Jesus.

Some people—most notably the religious professionals—said Jesus was an imposter. Some said Jesus was another in the long line of Jewish prophets. These were the people who benefited from his miracles and listened intently to his teaching. Some thought Jesus was John the Baptist come back to life—a foolish notion to Peter since he had known them both. Some thought Jesus would turn out to be a Messiah in the style of David who would raise an army and get Rome off their Jewish backs. This idea attracted many zealots and potential guerrilla fighters. Peter had sorted through public opinion and firmly decided that Jesus was to be, not his national hero, but his Savior—a decision that even now makes enemies of those who wish him to be less.

There is no decision like those studied decisions that we arrive at on our own. We stand for them as we could never stand for mere hearsay.

PRAYER
*Lord, I agree with Peter. I also confess that you
are the Christ, the Son of the living God.*

CHAPTER TWELVE

THE YEAST OF
THE PHARISEES AND
THE SADDUCEES

The Pharisees and Sadducees approached, and as a test, asked Him to show them a sign from heaven.

² He answered them: "When evening comes you say, 'It will be good weather, because the sky is red.' ³ And in the morning, 'Today will be stormy because the sky is red and threatening.' You know how to read the appearance of the sky, but you can't read the signs of the times. ⁴ An evil and adulterous generation wants a sign, but no sign will be given to it except the sign of Jonah." Then He left them and went away.

⁵ When the disciples reached the other shore, they had forgotten to take bread.

⁶ Then Jesus told them, "Watch out and beware of the yeast of the Pharisees and Sadducees."

⁷ And they discussed among themselves, "We didn't bring any bread!"

[8] Aware of this, Jesus said, "You of little faith! Why are you discussing among yourselves that you do not have bread? [9] Don't you understand yet? Don't you remember the five loaves for the five thousand and how many baskets you collected? [10] Or the seven loaves for the four thousand and how many large baskets you collected? [11] Why is it you don't understand that when I told you, 'Beware of the yeast of the Pharisees and Sadducees,' it wasn't about bread?" [12] Then they understood that He did not tell them to beware of the yeast in bread, but of the teaching of the Pharisees and Sadducees.

PETER'S CONFESSION OF THE MESSIAH

[13] When Jesus came to the region of Caesarea Philippi, He asked His disciples, "Who do people say that the Son of Man is?"

[14] And they said, "Some say John the Baptist; others, Elijah; still others, Jeremiah or one of the prophets."

[15] "But you," He asked them, "who do you say that I am?"

[16] Simon Peter answered, "You are the Messiah, the Son of the living God!"

[17] And Jesus responded, "Blessed are you, Simon son of Jonah, because flesh and blood did not reveal this to you, but My Father in heaven. [18] And I also say to you that you are Peter, and on this rock I will build My church, and the forces of Hades will not overpower it. [19] I will give you the keys of the kingdom of heaven, and whatever you bind on earth will have been bound in heaven, and whatever you loose on earth will have been loosed in heaven."

[20] And He gave the disciples orders to tell no one that He was the Messiah.

HIS DEATH AND RESURRECTION PREDICTED

[21] From then on Jesus began to point out to His disciples that He must go to Jerusalem and suffer many things from the elders, chief priests, and scribes, be killed, and be raised the third day. [22] Then Peter took Him aside and began to rebuke Him, "Oh no, Lord! This will never happen to You!"

[23] But He turned and told Peter, "Get behind Me, Satan! You are an offense to Me, because you're not thinking about God's concerns, but man's."

TAKE UP YOUR CROSS

[24] Then Jesus said to His disciples, "If anyone wants to come with Me, he must deny himself, take up his cross, and follow Me. [25] For whoever wants to save his life will lose it, but whoever loses his life because of Me will find it. [26] What will it benefit a man if he gains the whole world yet loses his life? Or what will a man give in exchange for his life? [27] For the Son of Man is going to come with His angels in the glory of His Father, and then He will reward each according to what he has done. [28] I assure you: There are some of those standing here who will not taste death until they see the Son of Man coming in His kingdom."

Then Peter said to Jesus, "Rabbi, it is good for us to be here! Let us make three taber-nacles: one for You, one for Moses, and one for Elijah"—because he did not know what he should say, since they were terrified.

God's Cherished Son
MARK 9:5

Peter's audacity amuses us. Moses, Elijah, and Jesus were talking, and Peter tried to get in the conversation. In rash exuberance, he interrupted Moses, Elijah, and Jesus. "Maybe we should try to build three little shrines where this great parley of the ages took place," said Peter. We cannot help but wonder why Peter thought he needed to get into the conversation.

What arrogance to think that Moses, Elijah, and Jesus were a part of his "bridge group." Did he really think these three giants of God's salvation plan would need his counsel on ways to advise God on how to finish up the plan of the ages? If you had asked him, "Peter, why did you join in?" what would he have said?

"Well, it just seems like at times a man's gotta speak his mind. I mean here we were, the four of us on the Mount of Transfiguration, and . . . "

"Excuse me, Peter, did you say the four of you?"

"Yeah, you know—me and Moses and Elijah and Jesus?"

"Yes, but did it not occur to you that sometimes you need simply to stand in awe of God?"

"Well, I just felt that I had to keep talking. It was all a little overwhelming, if you know what I mean."

We are not told whether Moses leaned over, cupped his fourteen-hundred-year-old hand to his mouth and said, "Jesus, who is this guy?"

Maybe Jesus whispered back to Moses, "Well, that's Peter. He's a little chatty, but some day he's going to lead the church into the age of the Spirit."

Moses must have shaken his head and said, "Are you sure you picked the right one? This guy looks more like a fisherman than a great leader."

"He is a fisherman," said Jesus, "but he'll improve with age."

The conference was never intended to be a meeting for four! Sometimes it's better to give God a little holy distance than to break into the throne room babbling with conversation.

PRAYER

Lord, sometimes I assume your holiness is but the preface to my chumminess. I can understand why Peter was so boisterous on the holy mountain. Help me to learn to see you high and lifted up and not assume I can jump into the center of your splendor with profane chatter.

CHAPTER THIRTEEN

FROM THE GOSPEL OF MARK, CHAPTER 9

T hen He said to them, "I assure you: There are some of those standing here who will not taste death until they see the kingdom of God come in power."

THE TRANSFIGURATION

² After six days Jesus took Peter, James, and John, and led them up on a high mountain by themselves to be alone. He was transformed in front of them, ³ and His clothes became dazzling, extremely white, as no launderer on earth could whiten them. ⁴ Elijah appeared to them with Moses, and they were talking with Jesus.

⁵ Then Peter said to Jesus, "Rabbi, it is good for us to be here! Let us make three tabernacles: one for You, one for Moses, and one for Elijah"— ⁶ because he did not know what he should say, since they were terrified.

⁷ A cloud appeared, overshadowing them, and a voice came from the cloud:

"This is My beloved Son;

Listen to Him!"

⁸ Then suddenly, looking around, they no longer saw anyone with them except Jesus alone.

⁹ As they were coming down from the mountain, He ordered them to tell no one what they had seen until the Son of Man had risen from the dead. ¹⁰ They kept this word to themselves, discussing what "rising from the dead" meant.

¹¹ Then they began to question Him, "Why do the scribes say that Elijah must come first?"

¹² "Elijah does come first and restores everything," He replied. "How then is it written about the Son of Man that He must suffer many things and be treated with contempt? ¹³ But I tell you that Elijah really has come, and they did to him whatever they wanted, just as it is written about him."

THE POWER OF FAITH OVER A DEMON

¹⁴ When they came to the disciples, they saw a large crowd around them and scribes disputing with them. ¹⁵ All of a sudden, when the whole crowd saw Him, they were amazed and ran to greet Him. ¹⁶ Then He asked them, "What are you arguing with them about?"

¹⁷ Out of the crowd, one man answered Him, "Teacher, I brought my son to You. He has a spirit that makes him unable to speak. ¹⁸ Wherever it seizes him, it throws him down, and he foams at the mouth, grinds his teeth, and becomes rigid. So I asked Your disciples to drive it out, but they couldn't."

¹⁹ He replied to them, "O, unbelieving generation! How long will I be with you? How long must I put up with you? Bring him

to Me." [20] So they brought him to Him. When the spirit saw Him, it immediately convulsed the boy. He fell to the ground and rolled around, foaming at the mouth. [21] "How long has this been happening to him?" Jesus asked his father.

"From childhood," he said. [22] "And many times it has thrown him into fire or water to destroy him. But if You can do anything, have compassion on us and help us."

[23] Then Jesus said to him, " 'If You can?' Everything is possible to the one who believes."

[24] Immediately the father of the boy cried out, "I do believe! Help my unbelief."

[25] When Jesus saw that a crowd was rapidly coming together, He rebuked the unclean spirit, saying to it, "You mute and deaf spirit, I command you: come out of him and never enter him again!"

[26] Then it came out, shrieking and convulsing him violently. The boy became like a corpse, so that many said, "He's dead." [27] But Jesus, taking him by the hand, raised him, and he stood up.

[28] After He went into a house, His disciples asked Him privately, "Why couldn't we drive it out?"

[29] And He told them, "This kind can come out by nothing but prayer (and fasting)."

THE SECOND PREDICTION OF HIS DEATH

[30] Then they left that place and made their way through Galilee, but He did not want anyone to know it. [31] For He was

teaching His disciples and telling them, "The Son of Man is being betrayed into the hands of men. They will kill Him, and after He is killed, He will rise three days later." [32] But they did not understand this statement, and they were afraid to ask Him.

WHO IS THE GREATEST?

[33] Then they came to Capernaum. When He was in the house, He asked them, "What were you arguing about on the way?" [34] But they were silent, because on the way they had been arguing with one another about who was the greatest. [35] Sitting down, He called the Twelve and said to them, "If anyone wants to be first, he must be last of all and servant of all." [36] Then He took a child, had him stand among them, and taking him in His arms, He said to them, [37] "Whoever welcomes one little child such as this in My name welcomes Me. And whoever welcomes Me does not welcome Me, but Him who sent Me."

IN HIS NAME

[38] John said to Him, "Teacher, we saw someone driving out demons in Your name, and we tried to stop him because he wasn't following us."

[39] "Don't stop him," said Jesus, "because there is no one who will perform a miracle in My name who can soon afterward speak evil of Me. [40] For whoever is not against us is for us. [41] And whoever gives you a cup of water to drink because of My name, since you belong to the Messiah—I assure you: He will never lose his reward.

WARNINGS FROM JESUS

[42] "But whoever causes the downfall of one of these little ones who believe in Me—it would be better for him if a heavy millstone were hung around his neck and he were thrown into the sea. [43] And if your hand causes your downfall, cut it off. It is better for you to enter life maimed than to have two hands and go to hell—the unquenchable fire, ([44] where

> Their worm does not die,
>
> and the fire is not quenched.)

[45] And if your foot causes your downfall, cut it off. It is better for you to enter life lame than to have two feet and be thrown into hell— (the unquenchable fire, [46] where

> Their worm does not die,
>
> and the fire is not quenched.)

[47] And if your eye causes your downfall, gouge it out. It is better for you to enter the kingdom of God with one eye than to have two eyes and be thrown into hell, [48] where

> Their worm does not die,
>
> and the fire is not quenched.

[49] For everyone will be salted with fire. [50] Salt is good, but if the salt should lose its flavor, how can you make it salty? Have salt among yourselves and be at peace with one another."

On the last and most important day of the festival, Jesus stood up and cried out, "If anyone is thirsty, he should come to Me and drink! The one who believes in Me, as the Scripture has said, will have streams of living water flow from deep within him."

Rivers of Living Water
JOHN 7:37-38

Here's to the thirst that fills us with Jesus! More than that, here's to the thirst that enables us to offer refreshing to someone else! Life in Christ supplies us with inward substance. Where Jesus indwells us, living waters flow out. How abundant is this living water? That all depends on how close the believer lives to Jesus and how consistently he or she walks with Jesus. For those who love Christ and spend a great deal of time in the relationship, the outflow can be impressive.

Ours is a barren world. The lives of many of the people around us are parched. They need times of refreshing. Most of the world is crushed to silence by two heavy questions: "Why was I ever born?" and "Where am I going?" The Christian knows. And that knowledge causes joy to visit the lost and leaves them with a compass.

Seek to be a person out of whose life flows the refreshing of Christ. The person filled with that outflowing river of living water can touch every part of their world with light and renewed perspective. From such a life, Christ flows outward and touches the unproductive with love and newness. From such a life, Christ flows to touch the disconsolate with joy. From such a life, the flow of living water washes away all grief with laughter. These flowing waters are in every way the grand refresher of the needy, thirsty world.

God's refreshing swims in the outflow of our obedience. From such a nourished soul, the arid world is touched with green. From that green, thirst is quenched. Meaning is served up in generous portions—ice cold—and life touches the dead.

God is still looking for persons who are willing to pay the price of devotion so their lives will be rivers of living water. Are you willing to be the channel of such a needy spring? Will you turn from your own pursuits to hunger after Christ? Will you spend the time with him that will furnish your life with such abundance of Spirit that many may turn to you and be refreshed?

PRAYER
Lord, I sometimes feel so dead and dry inside. May I walk with you until I feel this wonderful inwardness of joy—a healing spring that you can use to gush out and deliver my soul and my world from this dryness.

CHAPTER FOURTEEN

THE UNBELIEF OF JESUS' BROTHERS

After this Jesus traveled in Galilee, since He did not want to travel in Judea because the Jews were trying to kill Him. ² The Jewish Festival of Tabernacles was near, ³ so His brothers said to Him, "Leave here and go to Judea so Your disciples can see Your works that You are doing. ⁴ For no one does anything in secret while he's seeking public recognition. If You do these things, show Yourself to the world." ⁵ (For not even His brothers believed in Him.)

⁶ Jesus told them, "My time has not yet arrived, but your time is always at hand. ⁷ The world cannot hate you, but it does hate Me because I testify about it—that its deeds are evil. ⁸ Go up to the festival yourselves. I'm not going up to the festival yet, because My time has not yet fully come." ⁹ After He had said these things, He stayed in Galilee.

JESUS AT THE FESTIVAL OF TABERNACLES

[10] When His brothers had gone up to the festival, then He also went up, not openly but secretly. [11] The Jews were looking for Him at the festival and saying, "Where is He?" [12] And there was a lot of discussion about Him among the crowds. Some were saying, "He's a good man." Others were saying, "No, on the contrary, He's deceiving the people." [13] Still, nobody was talking publicly about Him because they feared the Jews.

[14] When the festival was already half over, Jesus went up into the temple complex and began to teach. [15] Then the Jews were amazed and said, "How does He know the Scriptures, since He hasn't been trained?"

[16] Jesus answered them, "My teaching isn't Mine, but is from the One who sent Me. [17] If anyone wants to do His will, he will understand whether the teaching is from God or if I am speaking on My own. [18] The one who speaks for himself seeks his own glory. But He who seeks the glory of the One who sent Him is true, and unrighteousness is not in Him. [19] Didn't Moses give you the law? Yet none of you keeps the law! Why do you want to kill Me?"

[20] "You have a demon!" the crowd responded. "Who wants to kill You?"

[21] "I did one work, and you are all amazed," Jesus answered. [22] "Consider this: Moses has given you circumcision—not that it comes from Moses but from the fathers—and you circumcise a man on the Sabbath. [23] If a man receives circumcision on the Sabbath so that the law of Moses won't be broken, are you angry at

Me because I made a man entirely well on the Sabbath? ²⁴ Stop judging according to outward appearances; rather judge according to righteous judgment."

THE IDENTITY OF THE MESSIAH

²⁵ Some of the people of Jerusalem were saying, "Isn't this the man they want to kill? ²⁶ Yet, look! He's speaking publicly and they're saying nothing to Him. Can it be true that the authorities know He is the Messiah? ²⁷ But we know where this man is from. When the Messiah comes, nobody will know where He is from."

²⁸ As He was teaching in the temple complex, Jesus cried out, "You know Me and you know where I am from. Yet I have not come on My own, but the One who sent Me is true. You don't know Him; ²⁹ I know Him because I am from Him, and He sent Me."

³⁰ Therefore they tried to seize Him. Yet no one laid a hand on Him because His hour had not yet come. ³¹ However, many from the crowd believed in Him and said, "When the Messiah comes, He won't perform more signs than this man has done, will He?"

³² The Pharisees heard the crowd muttering these things about Him, so the chief priests and the Pharisees sent temple police to arrest Him.

³³ Therefore Jesus said, "I am only with you for a short time. Then I'm going to the One who sent Me. ³⁴ You will look for Me, and you will not find Me; and where I am, you cannot come."

³⁵ Then the Jews said to one another, "Where does He intend to go so we won't find Him? He doesn't intend to go to the

Dispersion among the Greeks and teach the Greeks, does He? [36] What is this remark He made: 'You will look for Me and you will not find Me; and where I am, you cannot come'?"

THE PROMISE OF THE SPIRIT

[37] On the last and most important day of the festival, Jesus stood up and cried out, "If anyone is thirsty, he should come to Me and drink! [38] The one who believes in Me, as the Scripture has said, will have streams of living water flow from deep within him." [39] He said this about the Spirit, whom those who believed in Him were going to receive, for the Spirit had not yet been received, because Jesus had not yet been glorified.

THE PEOPLE ARE DIVIDED OVER JESUS

[40] When some from the crowd heard these words, they said, "This really is the Prophet!" [41] Others said, "This is the Messiah!" But some said, "Surely the Messiah doesn't come from Galilee, does He? [42] Doesn't the Scripture say that the Messiah comes from David's offspring and from the town of Bethlehem, where David once lived?" [43] So a division occurred among the crowd because of Him. [44] Some of them wanted to seize Him, but no one laid hands on Him.

DEBATE OVER JESUS' CLAIMS

[45] Then the temple police came to the chief priests and Pharisees, who asked them, "Why haven't you brought Him?"

⁴⁶ The police answered, "No man ever spoke like this!"

⁴⁷ Then the Pharisees responded to them: "Are you fooled too? ⁴⁸ Have any of the rulers believed in Him? Or any of the Pharisees? ⁴⁹ But this crowd, which doesn't know the law, is accursed!"

⁵⁰ Nicodemus—the one who came to Him previously, being one of them—said to them, ⁵¹ "Our law doesn't judge a man before it hears from him and knows what he's doing, does it?"

⁵² "You aren't from Galilee too, are you?" they replied. "Search and see: no prophet arises from Galilee."

"Woe to you! You build monuments to the prophets, and your fathers killed them."

The Unknown Hypocrite

LUKE 11:47

Are you guilty of the sin called "godly chronocentrism"? This is the disease of believing we are more enlightened than the generations that preceded us. Have you not heard people say, "If I had been living in Jesus' day, I surely would not have crucified him." Most people who would say that have never done one thing to stop racial oppression in their own city. They have done little to help the handicapped or serve in the soup lines of the community. Yet they are convinced they really are noble. They truly believe if they had been given a shot at that first Good Friday, they would have protected Christ from Pilate's abuse.

It is likely not true. The Pharisees of Jesus' day made a martyr out of Jesus. Their collective fury about his teachings would soon hang him by his hands in the winds of April. Yet if you mentioned any of Israel's past prophets, they would get all misty eyed and say, "Well, if we had been alive in his day, we surely would not have hanged him in the square or imprisoned him in a horrible dungeon."

Good people create crucifixions. And they always believe they are doing God service when they do. Who could have been better than the Pharisees? They had all but memorized the Old Testament. They were big on theology. They never caused trouble in the community. They gave 10 percent to the temple. You could count on them to make sure that God's Word was always strictly interpreted. In a way, a part of the animosity they spent on Jesus came from their noble drive to be sure that no false Messiah ever deceived the people and led them astray.

Jesus was frank with the Pharisees. They thought they were more holy than their fathers, but they were no different from the generations that preceded them. Their forebears also laid wreaths at the tomb of those prophets whom their grandfathers had killed. And so it goes! The travesty begins by believing we are more holy and more insightful than yesterday's believers. Ask God for sight, and be careful lest you come to believe you are better than you really are.

PRAYER
Lord, I am no better than those who came before me.
May I be as good as some of them were.

CHAPTER FIFTEEN

THE MODEL PRAYER

He was praying in a certain place, and when He finished, one of His disciples said to Him, "Lord, teach us to pray, just as John also taught his disciples."

² He said to them, "Whenever you pray, say:

> Father, Your name be honored as holy.
> Your kingdom come.
> ³ Give us each day our daily bread.
> ⁴ And forgive us our sins,
> for we ourselves also forgive everyone
> in debt to us.
> And do not bring us into temptation."

KEEP ASKING, SEARCHING, KNOCKING

⁵ He also said to them: "Suppose one of you has a friend and goes to him at midnight and says to him, 'Friend, lend me three loaves of bread, ⁶ because a friend

of mine on a journey has come to me, and I don't have anything to offer him.' ⁷ Then he will answer from inside and say, 'Don't bother me! The door is already locked, and my children and I have gone to bed. I can't get up to give you anything.' ⁸ I tell you, even though he won't get up and give him anything because he is his friend, yet because of his persistence, he will get up and give him as much as he needs.

⁹ "So I say to you, keep asking, and it will be given to you. Keep searching, and you will find. Keep knocking, and the door will be opened to you. ¹⁰ For everyone who asks receives, and the one who searches finds, and to the one who knocks, the door will be opened. ¹¹ What father among you, if his son asks for a fish, will, instead of a fish, give him a snake? ¹² Or if he asks for an egg, will give him a scorpion? ¹³ If you then, who are evil, know how to give good gifts to your children, how much more will the heavenly Father give the Holy Spirit to those who ask Him?"

A HOUSE DIVIDED

¹⁴ Now He was driving out a demon that was mute. When the demon came out, the man spoke who had been unable to speak, and the crowds were amazed. ¹⁵ But some of them said, "He drives out demons by Beelzebul, the ruler of the demons!" ¹⁶ And others, as a test, were demanding of Him a sign from heaven.

¹⁷ Knowing their thoughts, He told them: "Every kingdom divided against itself is headed for destruction, and a house divided

against itself falls. [18] If Satan also is divided against himself, how will his kingdom stand? For you say I drive out demons by Beelzebul. [19] And if I drive out demons by Beelzebul, by whom do your sons drive them out? For this reason they will be your judges. [20] If I drive out demons by the finger of God, then the kingdom of God has come to you. [21] When a strong man, fully armed, guards his estate, his possessions are secure. [22] But when one stronger than he attacks and overpowers him, he takes from him all his weapons in which he trusted, and divides up his plunder. [23] Anyone who is not with Me is against Me, and anyone who does not gather with Me scatters.

AN UNCLEAN SPIRIT'S RETURN

[24] "When an unclean spirit comes out of a man, it roams through waterless places looking for rest, and not finding rest, it then says, 'I'll go back to my house where I came from.' [25] And returning, it finds the house swept and put in order. [26] Then off it goes and brings seven other spirits more evil than itself, and they enter and settle down there. As a result, that man's last condition is worse than the first."

TRUE BLESSEDNESS

[27] As He was saying these things, a woman from the crowd raised her voice and said to Him, "Blessed is the womb that bore You, and the breasts that nursed You!"

²⁸ He said, "More blessed still are those who hear the word of God and keep it!"

THE SIGN OF JONAH

²⁹ As the crowds were increasing, He began saying: "This generation is an evil generation. It demands a sign, but no sign will be given to it except the sign of Jonah. ³⁰ For just as Jonah became a sign to the people of Nineveh, so also the Son of Man will be to this generation. ³¹ The queen of the south will rise up at the judgment with the men of this generation and condemn them, because she came from the ends of the earth to hear the wisdom of Solomon; and look—something greater than Solomon is here! ³² The men of Nineveh will rise up at the judgment with this generation and condemn it, because they repented at Jonah's proclamation; and look—something greater than Jonah is here!

THE LAMP OF THE BODY

³³ "No one lights a lamp and puts it in the cellar or under a basket, but on a lampstand, so that those who come in may see its light. ³⁴ Your eye is the lamp of the body. When your eye is good, your whole body is also full of light. But when it is bad, your body is also full of darkness. ³⁵ Take care then, that the light in you is not darkness. ³⁶ If therefore your whole body is full of light, with no part of it in darkness, the whole body will be full of light, as when a lamp shines its light on you."

RELIGIOUS HYPOCRISY DENOUNCED

37 As He was speaking, a Pharisee asked Him to dine with him. So He went in and reclined at the table. 38 When the Pharisee saw this, he was amazed that He did not first perform the ritual washing before dinner. 39 But the Lord said to him: "Now you Pharisees clean the outside of the cup and dish, but inside you are full of greed and evil. 40 Fools! Didn't He who made the outside make the inside too? 41 But give to charity what is within, and then everything is clean for you.

42 "But woe to you Pharisees! You give a tenth of mint, rue, and every kind of herb, and you bypass justice and love for God. These things you should have done without neglecting the others.

43 "Woe to you Pharisees! You love the front seat in the synagogues and greetings in the marketplaces.

44 "Woe to you! You are like unmarked graves; the people who walk over them don't know it."

45 One of the experts in the law answered Him, "Teacher, when You say these things You insult us too."

46 And He said: "Woe to you experts in the law as well! You load people with burdens that are hard to carry, yet you yourselves don't touch these burdens with one of your fingers.

47 "Woe to you! You build monuments to the prophets, and your fathers killed them. 48 Therefore you are witnesses that you approve the deeds of your fathers, for they killed them, and you

build their monuments. [49] And because of this, the wisdom of God said, 'I will send them prophets and apostles, and some of them they will kill and persecute,' [50] so that this generation may be held responsible for the blood of all the prophets shed since the foundation of the world, [51] from the blood of Abel to the blood of Zechariah, who perished between the altar and the sanctuary.

"Yes, I tell you, this generation will be held responsible.

[52] "Woe to you experts in the law! You have taken away the key of knowledge! You didn't go in yourselves, and you hindered those who were going in."

[53] When He left there, the scribes and the Pharisees began to oppose Him fiercely and to cross-examine Him about many things; [54] they were lying in wait for Him to trap Him in something He said.

The Transfiguration

The throne has ordered council. Moses comes to say the Law shall still remain unchanged. Though heaven and earth shall pass away, the ten words of Sinai shall be the moral rule of every age.

Elijah comes as an ambassador of all the prophets. Hear him thunder God's Torah to Israel and before the thunder of his voice has died away, you will hear the lament of Jeremiah and the timeless poems of Isaiah.

"Here," says Moses, "is the Law of God; I carried it down an ancient mountain that the world might live better." "Here," says Jesus, "are my hands, that the world might know how much God loves it."

The other two beheld Christ's hands and laid the law and timeless scroll before a simple carpenter and fell upon their knees and wept.

Raffaello Santi (1483-1520) is known as one of the finest portraitists of the Renaissance. The pictorial narrative he chose for this piece depicts several episodes surrounding the central event, and showcases his artistic ability with the looks on the characters' faces.

His disciples questioned Him: "Rabbi, who sinned, this man or his parents, that he was born blind?" "Neither this man sinned nor his parents," Jesus answered. "This came about so that God's works might be displayed in him."

Birth Defects

JOHN 9:2-3

We are always looking for answers to those problems we cannot understand. When we see any life or situation malformed, we cry out to God, "Who's responsible for this?" "Why did this happen?" Usually the question implies one of two answers. Did God do this? or did Satan do this? In this case, the issue was put to Jesus. "Who sinned, this man or his parents, that he was born blind?"

Jesus did not assign the birth defect to either God or the devil. Neither the man nor his parents were to take the rap for his unfortunate condition. The origin of some unexplainable horrors may not be easily defined. Perhaps the terror itself may be used of God in some less tangible way to bless the world. The man's condition could only be explained as a possible demonstration of the power of God.

Have you not known someone whose handicap fell upon them with a vengeance? No one knew why, and yet their handicap produced a life of great influence that never would have come to be without their seemingly unjust handicap.

Helen Keller blessed the world with a wisdom that grew from being deaf and blind. Dostoyevsky's epilepsy may have moved him from mediocrity to genius. Would Beethoven have been as brilliant without his deafness? Who can say? Cervantes was an amputee. His challenge may have given him his literary clout. Whitman sang from a wheelchair. Elizabeth Barrett grew strong from her invalid years. Steven Hawking defined the universe from the midst of an immense handicap. And Jesus was never more effective than when he hung on a cross.

So the question is pondered: "Who sinned, this man or his parents?"

But the point is elsewhere, said Jesus. Man's questions are no match for God's mysteries. He was about to be glorified—draw attention to himself, his power, his mercy—through one man's handicap. The man born blind would find himself and his story recorded in the world's best-selling book. He would teach the world for the next twenty centuries all that God can do with impossible situations.

PRAYER

Lord, we are all handicapped. We are all illustrations of what you can do with just a bit of surrender and a dab of honest need.

CHAPTER SIXTEEN

THE SIXTH SIGN: HEALING
A MAN BORN BLIND

As He was passing by, He saw a man blind from birth. [2] His disciples questioned Him: "Rabbi, who sinned, this man or his parents, that he was born blind?"

[3] "Neither this man sinned nor his parents," Jesus answered. "This came about so that God's works might be displayed in him. [4] We must do the works of Him who sent Me while it is day. Night is coming when no one can work. [5] As long as I am in the world, I am the light of the world."

[6] After He said these things He spit on the ground, made some mud from the saliva, and spread the mud on his eyes. [7] "Go," He told him, "wash in the pool of Siloam" (which means "Sent"). So he left, washed, and came back seeing.

⁸ His neighbors and those who formerly had seen him as a beggar said, "Isn't this the man who sat begging?" ⁹ Some said, "He's the one." "No," others were saying, "but he looks like him."

He kept saying, "I'm the one!"

¹⁰ Therefore they asked him, "Then how were your eyes opened?"

¹¹ He answered, "The man called Jesus made mud, spread it on my eyes, and told me, 'Go to Siloam and wash.' So when I went and washed I received my sight."

¹² "Where is He?" they asked.

"I don't know," he said.

THE HEALED MAN'S TESTIMONY

¹³ They brought to the Pharisees the man who used to be blind. ¹⁴ The day that Jesus made the mud and opened his eyes was a Sabbath. ¹⁵ So again the Pharisees asked him how he received his sight.

"He put mud on my eyes," he told them. "I washed and I can see."

¹⁶ Therefore some of the Pharisees said, "This man is not from God, for He doesn't keep the Sabbath!" But others were saying, "How can a sinful man perform such signs?" And there was a division among them.

¹⁷ Again they asked the blind man, "What do you say about Him, since He opened your eyes?"

"He's a prophet," he said.

¹⁸ The Jews did not believe this about him—that he was blind and received sight—until they summoned the parents of the one who had received his sight.

¹⁹ They asked them, "Is this your son, whom you say was born blind? How then does he now see?"

²⁰ "We know this is our son and that he was born blind," his parents answered. ²¹ "But we don't know how he now sees, and we don't know who opened his eyes. Ask him; he's of age. He will speak for himself." ²² His parents said these things because they were afraid of the Jews, since the Jews had already agreed that if anyone confessed Him as Messiah, he would be banned from the synagogue. ²³ This is why his parents said, "He's of age; ask him."

²⁴ So a second time they summoned the man who had been blind and told him, "Give glory to God. We know that this man is a sinner!"

²⁵ He answered, "Whether or not He's a sinner, I don't know. One thing I do know: I was blind, and now I can see!"

²⁶ Then they asked him, "What did He do to you? How did He open your eyes?"

²⁷ "I already told you," he said, "and you didn't listen. Why do you want to hear it again? You don't want to become His disciples too, do you?"

²⁸ They ridiculed him: "You're that man's disciple, but we're Moses' disciples. ²⁹ We know that God has spoken to Moses. But this man—we don't know where He's from!"

³⁰ "This is an amazing thing," the man told them. "You don't know where He is from; yet He opened my eyes! ³¹ We know that

God doesn't listen to sinners; but if anyone is God-fearing and does His will, He listens to him. [32] Throughout history no one has ever heard of someone opening the eyes of a person born blind. [33] If this man were not from God, He wouldn't be able to do anything."

[34] "You were born entirely in sin," they replied, "and are you trying to teach us?" Then they threw him out.

THE BLIND MAN'S SIGHT AND THE PHARISEES' BLINDNESS

[35] When Jesus heard that they had thrown the man out, He found him and asked, "Do you believe in the Son of Man?"

[36] "Who is He, Sir, that I may believe in Him?" he asked in return.

[37] Jesus answered, "You have both seen Him and He is the One speaking with you."

[38] "I believe, Lord!" he said, and he worshiped Him.

[39] Jesus said, "I came into this world for judgment, in order that those who do not see may see and those who do see may become blind."

[40] Some of the Pharisees who were with Him heard these things and asked Him, "We aren't blind too, are we?"

[41] "If you were blind," Jesus told them, "you wouldn't have sin. But now that you say, 'We see'—your sin remains."

Christ Seats the Child in the Midst of the Disciples

Small wonder Jesus blessed the children; it was easy to bless what he once was. So he took them in his arms and remembered that he once knew such embraces when he ran into the circle of Mary's consolation. He could easily bless what he had been — a child, so that once in time, for all time, the world would marvel that God, knowing all things, knew best how to be a child.

The Book of Jesus, Edited by Calvin Miller, pp. 143-144

Preti seems to be focusing Christ's attention on the viewers instead of the child, which seems to match the inference of Mark 9:37. Such an interpretation may be confirmed by Jesus' uplifted hand, which seems to be pointing heavenward to the Father.

"A thief comes only to steal and to kill and to destroy. I have come that they may have life and have it in abundance."

I Am the Only Portal
JOHN 10:10

How can you tell a true Messiah from a false one? A true Messiah lives to bless his followers. A false messiah comes to be blessed by his followers.

A true Messiah dies for his followers; a false messiah leads his children to drink poison kool-aid.

A true Messiah says he's coming again; a false messiah asks his children to catch a rocket ship or a comet to escape earth.

A true Messiah denies himself the pleasure of having a family. A false messiah takes many wives.

A true Messiah says, "Honor the heritage of truth." A false messiah says, "The only important truth is 'new' truth, and all truth begins with me."

A true Messiah serves his followers; the false messiah is served by them.

A true Messiah washes feet; a false messiah wants his followers to wash his feet.

Jesus said that many "thieves" would come and break into the fold of God. They would steal the elect—the faith of the elect—and build a following from those who trusted their deception. Jesus claimed that he had come to bring abundant life to all who trusted him.

What does this abundant life contain? Peace of mind, yes—but more than that. Does it contain that odd but warm euphoria? Yes! That sense of moral enhancement? That wonderful lightness of being? Does this abundant life not promise us a grand completion? Yes! When this life is over, we cannot think of anything very significant that we would like to have that is not already ours. We are complete in Christ, lavishly furnished with eternity and time.

An infallible road map leads us to the Author of eternal life. Since the Author of the map is the Author of salvation, we may be sure that the Scriptures bring us to the Savior they were written to exalt—the One who owns us, loves us, and has given us the key to the family vault. This true Messiah says to us, "Inherit the earth! Stake a claim on heaven! Live in joy—all things are yours!"

PRAYER
Lord, you are the door. Let me enter spiritual fullness through you. You are abundance. Help me lay by my poverty and indulge myself in joy.

CHAPTER SEVENTEEN

THE IDEAL SHEPHERD

"I assure you: Anyone who doesn't enter the sheep pen by the door, but climbs in some other way, is a thief and a robber. 2 The one who enters by the door is the shepherd of the sheep. 3 The doorkeeper opens it for him, and the sheep hear his voice. He calls his own sheep by name and leads them out. 4 When he has brought all his own outside, he goes ahead of them. The sheep follow him because they recognize his voice. 5 They will never follow a stranger; instead they will run away from him, because they don't recognize the voice of strangers."

6 Jesus gave them this illustration, but they did not understand what He was telling them.

THE GOOD SHEPHERD

7 So Jesus said again, "I assure you: I am the door of the sheep. 8 All who came before Me are thieves and robbers, but the sheep didn't listen to them. 9 I am the door. If anyone enters by Me, he will be saved, and will

come in and go out and find pasture. [10] A thief comes only to steal and to kill and to destroy. I have come that they may have life and have it in abundance.

[11] "I am the good shepherd. The good shepherd lays down His life for the sheep. [12] The hired man, since he's not the shepherd and doesn't own the sheep, leaves them and runs away when he sees a wolf coming. The wolf then snatches and scatters them. [13] This happens because he is a hired man and doesn't care about the sheep.

[14] "I am the good shepherd. I know My own sheep, and they know Me, [15] as the Father knows Me, and I know the Father. I lay down My life for the sheep. [16] But I have other sheep that are not of this fold; I must bring them also, and they will listen to My voice. Then there will be one flock, one shepherd. [17] This is why the Father loves Me, because I am laying down My life that I may take it up again. [18] No one takes it from Me, but I lay it down on My own. I have the right to lay it down and I have the right to take it up again. I have received this command from My Father."

[19] Again a division took place among the Jews because of these words. [20] Many of them were saying, "He has a demon and He's crazy! Why do you listen to Him?" [21] Others were saying, "These aren't the words of someone demon-possessed. Can a demon open the eyes of the blind?"

JESUS AT THE FESTIVAL OF DEDICATION

²² Then the Festival of Dedication took place in Jerusalem; and it was winter. ²³ Jesus was walking in the temple complex in Solomon's Colonnade. ²⁴ Then the Jews surrounded Him and asked, "How long are you going to keep us in suspense? If You are the Messiah, tell us plainly."

²⁵ "I did tell you and you don't believe," Jesus answered them. "The works that I do in My Father's name testify about Me. ²⁶ But you don't believe because you are not My sheep. ²⁷ My sheep hear My voice, I know them, and they follow Me. ²⁸ I give them eternal life, and they will never perish—ever! No one will snatch them out of My hand. ²⁹ My Father, who has given them to Me, is greater than all. No one is able to snatch them out of the Father's hand. ³⁰ The Father and I are one."

RENEWED EFFORTS TO STONE JESUS

³¹ Again the Jews picked up rocks to stone Him.

³² Jesus replied, "I have shown you many good works from the Father. For which of these works are you stoning Me?"

³³ "We aren't stoning You for a good work," the Jews answered, "but for blasphemy, and because You—being a man—make Yourself God."

[34] Jesus answered them, "Isn't it written in your law, 'I said, you are gods'? [35] If He called those to whom the word of God came 'gods'—and the Scripture cannot be broken— [36] do you say, 'You are blaspheming' to the One the Father set apart and sent into the world, because I said 'I am the Son of God'? [37] If I am not doing My Father's works, don't believe Me. [38] But if I am doing them and you don't believe Me, believe the works. This way you will know and understand that the Father is in Me and I in the Father." [39] Then they were trying again to seize Him, yet He eluded their grasp.

MANY BEYOND THE JORDAN BELIEVE IN JESUS

[40] So He departed again across the Jordan to the place where John first was baptizing, and He remained there. [41] Many came to Him and said, "John never did a sign, but everything John said about this man was true." [42] And many believed in Him there.

Salvator Mundi

Stand there, Savior, on the edge of worlds!
Hold out the globe, which ever was your passion!
The world is round, and fits — a tiny thing —
   into that wide emptiness
   that only you could ever fill.
Yet in your day, there was no globe.
The brightest men supposed the world flat.
And all of those who sailed past the Pillars of
   Hercules
Would sail beyond the edge and be forever lost.
How much we owe you for holding
   our poor, uninformed planet in your hand
Until our petty, grasping ignorance
   could mature enough to call you Lord.

Calvin Miller, From *My Journal*

Osorio (c. 1640-1721) presents Christ as a cosmic redeemer, holding the world in his left hand and raising his right hand to bless and restore it. Osorio paints the earth a monotonous gray, which we assume will blaze with form and color at Christ's redemptive touch.

"I'll get up, go to my father, and say to him, 'Father, I have sinned against heaven and in your sight. I'm no longer worthy to be called your son. Make me like one of your hired hands.'"

The Supremacy of Need

LUKE 15:18-19

I must confess I need you. I gave up every hint of self-sufficiency long ago. Some say my faith is only the crutch of a weak man. I don't object to the idea, but the word *crutch* is too weak a word. Crutches only prop up the infirm. I am in need of a sustainer, not a crutch.

Need is my friend and not my enemy. It was need that long ago caused me to turn to you. I wish I had done it earlier. I struggled so long trying to be self-sufficient, trying to make my own way. When the walls of my life were crumbling faster than I could prop them up, I found you. I knew you would do me no good until I surrendered my own attempt to repair things and said very honestly, "I need you!"

The prodigal son learned a lesson in the pigpen which a person can never pick up in finishing school. He began to be in need. And need—like an old friend—came to him, sat with him, and reminded him that all his self-sufficiency was being consumed on the low altar of his stubborn pride. Need caused him to remember his father. Salvation drew him homeward, but need was his counselor on the journey.

Need is the hardest kind of dependency for us to confess. Why? Because all of our lives we struggle to become financially independent. We struggle to be self-sufficient. The word *needy* has come to be a word referring to the economically depressed, the indigent, the poverty stricken, the street sleepers. Fearing the needy category, we are taught to save, to invest, to work hard, to buy life insurance.

Now when we are almost there . . . now when we are all but financially free, we are taught to seek what all of our lives we have tried to escape: spiritual neediness. Still it is the beginning of all reality: the reality that Christ provides. So we turn to him. His sufficiency meets our insufficiency, and we are healed. At long last, we bless the word we so long tried to avoid: *neediness.* In this word is hidden life in Christ and, therefore, all things.

PRAYER
Lord, I need you. I'm glad. Life never goes well when I don't.

CHAPTER EIGHTEEN

FROM THE GOSPEL OF LUKE, CHAPTER 15

THE PARABLE OF
THE LOST SHEEP

All the tax collectors and sinners were drawing near to listen to Him. ² And the Pharisees and scribes were complaining, "This man welcomes sinners and eats with them!"

³ So He told them this parable: ⁴ "What man among you, who has a hundred sheep and loses one of them, does not leave the ninety-nine in the open field and go after the lost one until he finds it? ⁵ When he has found it, he joyfully puts it on his shoulders, ⁶ and coming home, he calls his friends and neighbors together, saying to them, 'Rejoice with me, because I have found my lost sheep!' ⁷ I tell you, in the same way, there will be more joy in heaven over one sinner who repents than over ninety-nine righteous people who don't need repentance.

THE PARABLE OF
THE LOST COIN

8 "Or what woman who has ten silver coins, if she loses one coin, does not light a lamp, sweep the house, and search carefully until she finds it? 9 When she finds it, she calls her women friends and neighbors together, saying, 'Rejoice with me, because I have found the silver coin I lost!' 10 I tell you, in the same way, there is joy in the presence of God's angels over one sinner who repents."

THE PARABLE OF THE LOST SON

11 He also said: "A man had two sons. 12 The younger of them said to his father, 'Father, give me the share of the estate I have coming to me.' So he distributed the assets to them. 13 Not many days later, the younger son gathered together all he had and traveled to a distant country, where he squandered his estate in foolish living. 14 After he had spent everything, a severe famine struck that country, and he had nothing. 15 Then he went to work for one of the citizens of that country, who sent him into his fields to feed pigs. 16 He longed to eat his fill from the carob pods the pigs were eating, and no one would give him any. 17 But when he came to his senses, he said, 'How many of my father's hired hands have more than enough food, and here I am dying of hunger! 18 I'll get up, go to my father, and say to him, "Father, I have sinned against heaven and in your sight. 19 I'm no longer worthy to be called your son. Make me like one of your hired hands." ' 20 So he got up and went to his father. But while the son was still a long way off, his father saw him and

was filled with compassion. He ran, threw his arms around his neck, and kissed him. ²¹ The son said to him, 'Father, I have sinned against heaven and in your sight. I'm no longer worthy to be called your son.'

²² "But the father told his slaves, 'Quick! Bring out the best robe and put it on him; put a ring on his finger and sandals on his feet. ²³ Then bring the fatted calf and slaughter it, and let's celebrate with a feast, ²⁴ because this son of mine was dead and is alive again; he was lost and is found!' So they began to celebrate.

²⁵ "Now his older son was in the field; as he came near the house, he heard music and dancing. ²⁶ So he summoned one of the servants and asked what these things meant. ²⁷ 'Your brother is here,' he told him, 'and your father has slaughtered the fatted calf because he has him back safe and sound.'

²⁸ "Then he became angry and didn't want to go in. So his father came out and pleaded with him. ²⁹ But he replied to his father, 'Look, I have been slaving many years for you, and I have never disobeyed your orders; yet you never gave me a young goat so I could celebrate with my friends. ³⁰ But when this son of yours came, who has devoured your assets with prostitutes, you slaughtered the fatted calf for him.'

³¹ " 'Son,' he said to him, 'you are always with me, and everything I have is yours. ³² But we had to celebrate and rejoice, because this brother of yours was dead and is alive again; he was lost and is found.' "

"The master praised the unrighteous manager because he had acted astutely. For the sons of this age are more astute than the sons of light in dealing with their own people."

One Eye on Tomorrow
LUKE 16:8

Not much can be said for the dishonest steward in Jesus' story except that he knew how to survive in his corrupt business. So why would Jesus compliment him? Well, Jesus did not compliment his corrupt business practices. Jesus was saying that those who live all their lives and never plan for eternity are even less wise than corrupt bookkeepers who may embezzle, but always have an eye on the future.

Always keep an eye on tomorrow, for today is not ultimate enough to mean anything, and yesterday is spent. Those who focus on yesterday we call traditionalists. Those who live for the moment we call momentary. Those who live for tomorrow we call the people of destiny. This is the category to be cherished by the people of God.

For additional proof, read Christ's story of the rich man and Lazarus in this chapter. Lazarus looked forward to heaven because he had no life or living here on earth. The rich man never thought much about heaven and probably went to hell because of that. People who go to heaven wind up there because heaven is dear to them. Heaven is dear to them because Christ dwells there. Their longing to see him face to face drives them toward the final place of grace.

Jesus spent much of his teaching time expounding on hell, a subject that has all but disappeared from the modern sermon. Yet hell is as real as heaven, and those who have always rejected faith have with each rejection made the choice of this awful place as their destiny. The tormented rich man wanted to save his brothers from such a place. He knew they would come to join him in hell one day. He knew they, too, had never found heaven in their hearts. Most of all, he heard the horrible truth that what we long for in life eventually owns us.

Eternity is real, and it is on the way. Living only for today is a lifestyle that cannot survive your lifetime. Plan to inherit eternal life. Move confidently toward your imperishable tomorrow.

PRAYER

Lord, may I awake every morning with the awareness that some great morning I'll wake in that land where morning lasts forever. To live without this awareness is to impose upon myself a voluntary darkness that can never know light.

CHAPTER NINETEEN

THE PARABLE OF THE DISHONEST MANAGER

He also said to the disciples: "There was a rich man who received an accusation that his manager was squandering his possessions. ² So he called the manager in and asked, 'What is this I hear about you? Give an account of your management, because you can no longer be my manager.'

³ "Then the manager said to himself, 'What should I do, since my master is taking the management away from me? I'm not strong enough to dig; I'm ashamed to beg. ⁴ I know what I'll do so that when I'm removed from management, people will welcome me into their homes.'

⁵ "So he summoned each one of his master's debtors. 'How much do you owe my master?' he asked the first one.

⁶ " 'A hundred measures of oil,' he said.

" 'Take your invoice,' he told him, 'sit down quickly, and write fifty.'

⁷ "Next he asked another, 'How much do you owe?'

" 'A hundred measures of wheat,' he said.

" 'Take your invoice,' he told him, 'and write eighty.'

⁸ "The master praised the unrighteous manager because he had acted astutely. For the sons of this age are more astute than the sons of light in dealing with their own people. ⁹ And I tell you, make friends for yourselves by means of the money of unrighteousness, so that when it fails, they may welcome you into eternal dwellings. ¹⁰ Whoever is faithful in very little is also faithful in much; and whoever is unrighteous in very little is also unrighteous in much. ¹¹ So if you have not been faithful with the unrighteous money, who will trust you with what is genuine? ¹² And if you have not been faithful with what belongs to someone else, who will give you what is your own? ¹³ No servant can be the slave of two masters, since either he will hate one and love the other, or he will be devoted to one and despise the other. You can't be slaves to both God and money."

KINGDOM VALUES

¹⁴ The Pharisees, who were lovers of money, were listening to all these things and scoffing at Him. ¹⁵ And He told them: "You are the ones who justify yourselves in the sight of others, but God knows your hearts. For what is highly admired by people is revolting in God's sight.

¹⁶ "The Law and the Prophets were until John; since then, the good news of the kingdom of God has been proclaimed, and everyone is strongly urged to enter it. ¹⁷ But it is easier for heaven and earth to pass away than for one stroke of a letter in the law to drop out.

¹⁸ "Everyone who divorces his wife and marries another woman commits adultery, and everyone who marries a woman divorced from her husband commits adultery.

THE RICH MAN AND LAZARUS

¹⁹ "There was a rich man who would dress in purple and fine linen, feasting lavishly every day. ²⁰ But at his gate was left a poor man named Lazarus, covered with sores. ²¹ He longed to be filled with what fell from the rich man's table, but instead the dogs would come and lick his sores. ²² One day the poor man died and was carried away by the angels to Abraham's side. The rich man also died and was buried. ²³ And being in torment in Hades, he looked up and saw Abraham a long way off, with Lazarus at his side. ²⁴ 'Father Abraham!' he called out, 'Have mercy on me and send Lazarus to dip the tip of his finger in water and cool my tongue, because I am in agony in this flame!'

²⁵ " 'Son,' Abraham said, 'remember that during your life you received your good things, just as Lazarus received bad things; but now he is comforted here, while you are in agony. ²⁶ Besides all this, a great chasm has been fixed between us and you, so that those who want to pass over from here to you cannot; neither can those from there cross over to us.'

²⁷ " 'Father,' he said, 'then I beg you to send him to my father's house— ²⁸ because I have five brothers—to warn them, so they won't also come to this place of torment.'

²⁹ "But Abraham said, 'They have Moses and the prophets; they should listen to them.'

³⁰ " 'No, Father Abraham,' he said. 'But if someone from the dead goes to them, they will repent.'

³¹ "But he told him, 'If they don't listen to Moses and the prophets, they will not be persuaded if someone rises from the dead.'"

Jesus wept. So the Jews said, "See how He loved him!" But some of them said, "Couldn't He who opened the blind man's eyes also have kept this man from dying?"

The Grief of God
JOHN 11:35-37

What made Jesus weep? Could it have been human faithlessness? Mary and Martha sorrowed so hopelessly in his presence. Here was Jesus, God's Son, for whom any miracle was possible, yet these women of Bethany protested as if nothing could be done. Here was needless human desperation standing right next to him who held the keys of death and hell. Could it be that Jesus weeps knowing that God is sovereign over all human heartache and we refuse to trust him?

What else made Jesus weep? Could it have been their slowness to understand that to be absent from the body is to be present with the Lord? Jesus was close to his own death. He knew that Lazarus was in a much better world than the one Mary and Martha wished he was still in. Jesus knew he was about to bring Lazarus back to the world at hand. Jesus knew he himself had left the ivory palaces of heaven to take up his dwelling among human beings. Now he must bring Lazarus—perhaps kicking and screaming—back to the world at hand. When anyone must leave the divine presence to return to earth, could it be that Jesus weeps? Perhaps Lazarus himself walked out of the tomb weeping.

What else made Jesus weep? Could it have been sheer grief? Jesus loved Lazarus as much as he despised the death. Thinking of Lazarus, he grieved his passing. This is the Christ who never lets human sorrow exist alone. This is the Christ about whom the prophet said, "Surely he has borne our grief and carried our sorrows."

One final thing must be said of Jesus' grief: He wept because he was part of our human condition. He was made in all ways like we are. Jesus did not enter our condition as the Son of God without tear ducts. He wept because he was human. He wept because we weep. He cried, and his tears prove that he became a real, emotional human being. Thus, we real, emotional human beings understand our similarities to the Savior.

PRAYER
Lord, thank you for weeping with Mary and Martha. It helps me to remember how much you despise death and how much I can depend on your tears when I must face my seasons of grief. Your joy is made full in my life when I remember that even when I hurt, heaven is capable of tears.

CHAPTER TWENTY

FROM THE GOSPEL OF JOHN, CHAPTER 11

LAZARUS DIES AT BETHANY

Now a man was sick, Lazarus from Bethany, the village of Mary and her sister Martha. [2] Mary was the one who anointed the Lord with fragrant oil and wiped His feet with her hair, and it was her brother Lazarus who was sick. [3] So the sisters sent a message to Him: "Lord, the one You love is sick."

[4] When Jesus heard it, He said, "This sickness will not end in death, but is for the glory of God, so that the Son of God may be glorified through it." [5] (Jesus loved Martha, her sister, and Lazarus.) [6] So when He heard that he was sick, He stayed two more days in the place where He was. [7] Then after that, He said to the disciples, "Let's go to Judea again."

[8] "Rabbi," the disciples told Him, "just now the Jews tried to stone You, and You're going there again?"

[9] "Aren't there twelve hours in a day?" Jesus answered. "If anyone walks during the day, he doesn't stumble, because he sees the light of this world. [10] If anyone walks during the night, he does stumble, because

the light is not in him." ¹¹ He said this, and then He told them, "Our friend Lazarus has fallen asleep, but I'm on My way to wake him up."

¹² Then the disciples said to Him, "Lord, if he has fallen asleep, he will get well."

¹³ Jesus, however, was speaking about his death, but they thought He was speaking about natural sleep. ¹⁴ So Jesus then told them plainly, "Lazarus has died. ¹⁵ I'm glad for you that I wasn't there, so that you may believe. But let's go to him."

¹⁶ Then Thomas (called "Twin") said to his fellow disciples, "Let's go so that we may die with Him."

THE RESURRECTION AND THE LIFE

¹⁷ When Jesus arrived, He found that Lazarus had already been in the tomb four days. ¹⁸ Bethany was near Jerusalem (about two miles away). ¹⁹ Many of the Jews had come to Martha and Mary to comfort them about their brother. ²⁰ As soon as Martha heard that Jesus was coming, she went to meet Him. But Mary remained seated in the house.

²¹ Then Martha said to Jesus, "Lord, if You had been here, my brother wouldn't have died. ²² Yet even now I know that whatever You ask from God, God will give You."

²³ "Your brother will rise again," Jesus told her.

²⁴ Martha said, "I know that he will rise again in the resurrection at the last day."

²⁵ Jesus said to her, "I am the resurrection and the life. The one who believes in Me, even if he dies, will live. ²⁶ Everyone who lives and believes in Me will never die—ever. Do you believe this?"

²⁷ "Yes, Lord," she told Him, "I believe You are the Messiah, the Son of God, who was to come into the world."

JESUS SHARES THE SORROW OF DEATH

²⁸ Having said this, she went back and called her sister Mary, saying in private, "The Teacher is here and is calling for you."

²⁹ As soon as she heard this, she got up quickly and went to Him. ³⁰ Jesus had not yet come into the village, but was still in the place where Martha had met Him. ³¹ The Jews who were with her in the house consoling her saw that Mary got up quickly and went out. So they followed her, supposing that she was going to the tomb to cry there.

³² When Mary came to where Jesus was and saw Him, she fell at His feet and told Him, "Lord, if You had been here, my brother would not have died!"

³³ When Jesus saw her crying, and the Jews who had come with her crying, He was angry in His spirit and deeply moved. ³⁴ "Where have you put him?" He asked.

"Lord," they told Him, "come and see."

³⁵ Jesus wept.

³⁶ So the Jews said, "See how He loved him!" ³⁷ But some of them said, "Couldn't He who opened the blind man's eyes also have kept this man from dying?"

THE SEVENTH SIGN: RAISING LAZARUS FROM THE DEAD

[38] Then Jesus, angry in Himself again, came to the tomb. It was a cave, and a stone was lying against it. [39] "Remove the stone," Jesus said.

Martha, the dead man's sister, told Him, "Lord, he already stinks. It's been four days."

[40] Jesus said to her, "Did I not tell you that if you believed you would see the glory of God?"

[41] So they removed the stone. Then Jesus raised His eyes and said, "Father, I thank You that You heard Me. [42] I know that You always hear Me, but because of the crowd standing here I said this, so they may believe You sent Me." [43] After He said this, He shouted with a loud voice, "Lazarus, come out!" [44] The dead man came out bound hand and foot with linen strips and with his face wrapped in a cloth. Jesus said to them, "Loose him and let him go."

THE PLOT TO KILL JESUS

[45] Therefore many of the Jews who came to Mary and saw what He did believed in Him. [46] But some of them went to the Pharisees and told them what Jesus had done.

[47] So the chief priests and the Pharisees convened the Sanhedrin and said, "What are we going to do since this man does many signs? [48] If we let Him continue in this way, everybody will

believe in Him! Then the Romans will come and remove both our place and our nation."

⁴⁹ One of them, Caiaphas, who was high priest that year, said to them, "You know nothing at all! ⁵⁰ You're not considering that it is to your advantage that one man should die for the people rather than the whole nation perish." ⁵¹ He did not say this on his own; but being high priest that year he prophesied that Jesus was going to die for the nation, ⁵² and not for the nation only, but also to unite the scattered children of God. ⁵³ So from that day on they plotted to kill Him. ⁵⁴ Therefore Jesus no longer walked openly among the Jews, but departed from there to the countryside near the wilderness, to a town called Ephraim. And He stayed there with the disciples.

⁵⁵ Now the Jewish Passover was near, and before the Passover many went up to Jerusalem from the country to purify themselves. ⁵⁶ They were looking for Jesus, and asking one another as they stood in the temple complex: "What do you think? He won't come to the festival, will He?"

⁵⁷ The chief priests and the Pharisees had given orders that if anyone knew where He was, he should report it so they could arrest Him.

"Whoever wants to become great among you must be your servant, and whoever wants to be first among you must be a slave to all. For even the Son of Man did not come to be served, but to serve, and to give His life—a ransom for many."

Pure Promotion
MARK 10:43-45

The lust for power is a universal appetite. Even before the cross, the humanity of human beings turned God's people into a common arena of power. James and John were saying to Jesus, "We want a special place in your kingdom, Lord. We want authority, recognition and power."

"Are you able?" asked Jesus, "to drink the cup I drink, or to be baptized with the baptism I am baptized with?"

James and John agreed that they were. They far overestimated their own ability to stand the rigors of Jesus' coming trial. Jesus pointed out their problem. Wanting his recognition and some wide arena of power, they were not schooled in the rigors of martyrdom.

Had James and John truly been able to drink his cup and be baptized with his baptism, five crosses—not just three—would have marked Calvary. Jesus' question points out that the kingdom of God is not a training camp for junior executives. Whoever wants to be first must be willing to be the last. Who wants to be master will gain that right by acting the part of a slave. Whoever wants to guarantee themselves a reigning position in heaven must find a way of dying on earth.

People like James and John are legion in the current kingdom. How often petty men and women struggle to have some office in the church. Many spend their entire lives trying to gain footholds of power in the religious and political arena. These cannot even be accused of seeking power in Jesus' coming kingdom. They want the power now. How these need to hear Jesus say once again, "Quit seeking political advantage. Quit using my church to glut your power appetite. Seek rather to drink my cup and be baptized with my baptism. Die for me, die with me, take up the dying life. After you've learned to die daily, we will talk about your position."

Oddly, those who submit themselves to die, who surrender any perceived rights to exert their influence over others, don't have any interest in ruling God's kingdom in heaven, since they were never really interested in ruling his kingdom on earth. They knew whose business that was.

PRAYER
Lord, I want to understand the dying life. I think it begins with losing all interest in what I might control and finding a vast interest in whom I might serve.

CHAPTER TWENTY-ONE

THE QUESTION OF DIVORCE

He set out from there and went to the region of Judea and across the Jordan. Then crowds converged on Him again and, as He usually did, He began teaching them once more. ² Some Pharisees approached Him to test Him. They asked, "Is it lawful for a man to divorce his wife?"

³ He replied to them, "What did Moses command you?"

⁴ They said, "Moses permitted us to write divorce papers and send her away."

⁵ But Jesus told them, "He wrote this command- ment for you because of the hardness of your hearts. ⁶ But from the beginning of creation God 'made them male and female':

⁷ 'For this reason a man will leave his
father and mother
(and be joined to his wife,)

⁸ and the two will become one flesh.'

So they are no longer two, but one flesh. [9] Therefore what God has joined together, man must not separate."

[10] Now in the house the disciples questioned Him again about this matter. [11] And He said to them, "Whoever divorces his wife and marries another commits adultery against her. [12] Also, if she divorces her husband and marries another, she commits adultery."

BLESSING THE CHILDREN

[13] Some people were bringing little children to Him so He might touch them. But His disciples rebuked them. [14] When Jesus saw it, He was indignant and said to them, "Let the little children come to Me; don't stop them, for the kingdom of God belongs to such as these. [15] I assure you: Whoever does not welcome the kingdom of God like a little child will never enter it." [16] After taking them in His arms, He laid His hands on them and blessed them.

THE RICH YOUNG RULER

[17] As He was going out on the road, a man ran up, knelt down before Him, and asked Him, "Good Teacher, what must I do to inherit eternal life?"

[18] But Jesus asked him, "Why do you call Me good? No one is good but One—God. [19] You know the commandments: 'Do not murder; do not commit adultery; do not steal; do not bear false witness; do not defraud; honor your father and mother.'"

[20] He said to Him, "Teacher, I have kept all these from my youth."

²¹ Then, looking at him, Jesus loved him and said to him, "You lack one thing: Go, sell all you have and give to the poor, and you will have treasure in heaven. Then come, follow Me." ²² But he was stunned at this demand, and he went away grieving, because he had many possessions.

POSSESSIONS AND THE KINGDOM

²³ Jesus looked around and said to His disciples, "How hard it is for those who have wealth to enter the kingdom of God!" ²⁴ But the disciples were astonished at His words. Again Jesus said to them, "Children, how hard it is to enter the kingdom of God! ²⁵ It is easier for a camel to go through the eye of a needle than for a rich person to enter the kingdom of God."

²⁶ But they were even more astonished, saying to one another, "Then who can be saved?"

²⁷ Looking at them, Jesus said, "With men it is impossible, but not with God, because all things are possible with God."

²⁸ Peter began to tell Him, "Look, we have left everything and followed You."

²⁹ "I assure you," Jesus said, "there is no one who has left house, brothers or sisters, mother or father, children, or fields because of Me and the gospel, ³⁰ who will not receive a hundred times more, now at this time—houses, brothers and sisters, mothers and children, and fields, with persecutions—and eternal life in the age to come. ³¹ But many who are first will be last, and the last first."

THE THIRD PREDICTION OF HIS DEATH

[32] They were on the road, going up to Jerusalem, and Jesus was walking ahead of them. They were astonished, but those who followed Him were afraid. And taking the Twelve aside again, He began to tell them the things that would happen to Him.

[33] "Listen! We are going up to Jerusalem. The Son of Man will be handed over to the chief priests and the scribes, and they will condemn Him to death. Then they will hand Him over to the Gentiles, [34] and they will mock Him, spit on Him, flog Him, and kill Him, and He will rise after three days."

SUFFERING AND SERVICE

[35] Then James and John, the sons of Zebedee, approached Him and said, "Teacher, we want You to do something for us if we ask You."

[36] "What do you want Me to do for you?" He asked them.

[37] "Grant us," they answered Him, "that we may sit at Your right and at Your left in Your glory."

[38] But Jesus said to them, "You don't know what you're asking. Are you able to drink the cup I drink, or to be baptized with the baptism I am baptized with?"

[39] "We are able," they told Him.

But Jesus said to them, "You will drink the cup I drink, and you will be baptized with the baptism I am baptized with. [40] But to sit at My right or left is not Mine to give, but it is for those for whom it has been prepared." ⁴¹ When the other ten disciples heard this, they began to be indignant with James and John.

⁴² And Jesus called them over and said to them, "You know that those who are regarded as rulers of the Gentiles dominate them, and their men of high positions exercise power over them. ⁴³ But it must not be like that among you. On the contrary, whoever wants to become great among you must be your servant, ⁴⁴ and whoever wants to be first among you must be a slave to all. ⁴⁵ For even the Son of Man did not come to be served, but to serve, and to give His life—a ransom for many."

A BLIND MAN HEALED

⁴⁶ They came to Jericho. And as He was leaving Jericho, and along with His disciples and a large crowd, Bartimaeus (the son of Timaeus), a blind beggar, was sitting by the road. ⁴⁷ When he heard that it was Jesus the Nazarene, he began to cry out, "Son of David, Jesus, have mercy on me!" ⁴⁸ Many people told him to keep quiet, but he was crying out all the more, "Have mercy on me, Son of David!"

⁴⁹ Jesus stopped and said, "Call him."

So they called the blind man and said to him, "Have courage! Get up; He's calling for you." ⁵⁰ He threw off his coat, jumped up, and came to Jesus.

⁵¹ Then Jesus answered him, "What do you want Me to do for you?"

"Rabbouni," the blind man told Him, "I want to see!"

⁵² "Go your way," Jesus told him. "Your faith has healed you." Immediately he could see, and began to follow Him on the road.

Now He came near the path down the Mount of Olives, and the whole crowd of the disciples began to praise God joyfully with a loud voice for all the miracles they had seen: "Blessed is the King who comes in the name of the Lord. Peace in heaven and glory in the highest heaven!"

The Last Hurrah!

LUKE 19:37-38

The last hurrah comes at the finale of all celebrations. Palm Sunday is unquestionably the last hurrah of the Christ. Four days later Jesus was in Gethsemane, and five days later he was on the cross. We must ask ourselves, "How could Jesus be both celebrated and condemned within the same five-day period." We must not assume that Jesus was so deluded by the wild Palm Sunday acclaim that the horrible condemnation of Friday surprised him. Never did Jesus say, "Father, I'm sure surprised at how fast my celebration turned into crucifixion."

Jesus knew the fickle nature of humankind. He understood how one may be a hero on Sunday and crucified on the following Friday. He held a fundamental distrust of the last hurrah.

So one important lesson for those who receive human acclaim today is to never assume that it will always be there. Yet the more challenging issue raised through Jesus' example is this: Can you trust others enough to freely serve them, knowing full well that they may turn on you tomorrow? For if you naively trust them, they may break your heart and leave you shattered in return for giving them your confidence. But that was Jesus' way. To love anyway.

Jesus loved Judas as much as he loved the other disciples, but he was not shattered when Judas betrayed him. He understood human nature but loved Judas anyway. How often we have disappointed God, and yet God is not destroyed by any of our momentary betrayals. He understands that we are human. He knows that sin camps so much in our lives that we cannot depend upon our own intentions.

Palm Sunday is evidence that we are to serve and even to receive the accolades of our friends. We are, however, always to remember that only God—and not anyone else—is perfect. Our friends may disappoint us. They may even crucify us. Nonetheless, they are loved by God. And we must love them even as they disappoint us, knowing that God loved us even as we disappointed him.

The love of the lovely is the way people love. The love of the unlovely is the way God loves.

PRAYER

Lord, knowing how fickle I am in my loving you, help me not to be debilitated when others who once praised me begin to betray me. Help me to remember that such love is really grace wearing another name.

CHAPTER TWENTY-TWO

FROM THE GOSPEL OF LUKE, CHAPTER 19

JESUS VISITS ZACCHAEUS

He entered Jericho and was passing through. ² There was a man named Zacchaeus who was a chief tax collector, and he was rich. ³ He was trying to see who Jesus was, but he was not able, in the crowd, because he was a short man. ⁴ So running ahead, he climbed up a sycamore tree to see Jesus, since He was about to pass that way. ⁵ When Jesus came to the place, He looked up and said to him, "Zacchaeus, hurry and come down, because today I must stay at your house."

⁶ So he quickly came down, and welcomed Him joyfully. ⁷ All who saw it began to complain, "He's gone to lodge with a sinful man!"

⁸ But Zacchaeus stood there and said to the Lord, "Look, I'll give half of my possessions to the poor, Lord! And if I have extorted anything from anyone, I'll pay back four times as much!"

⁹ "Today salvation has come to this house," Jesus told him, "because he too is a son of Abraham. ¹⁰ For the Son of Man has come to seek and to save the lost."

THE PARABLE OF THE TEN MINAS

[11] As they were listening to this, He went on to tell a parable, because He was near Jerusalem, and they thought the kingdom of God was going to appear right away.

[12] Therefore He said: "A nobleman traveled to a far country to receive for himself authority to be king, and then return; [13] and having called ten of his slaves, he gave them ten minas and told them, 'Do business until I come back.'

[14] "But his subjects hated him, and sent a delegation after him, saying, 'We don't want this man to rule over us!'

[15] "At his return, having received the authority to be king, he summoned those slaves to whom he had given the money so that he could find out how much they had made in business. [16] The first came forward and said, 'Master, your mina has earned ten more minas.'

[17] " 'Well done, good slave!' he told him. 'Because you have been faithful in a very small matter, have authority over ten towns.'

[18] "The second came and said, 'Master, your mina has made five minas.'

[19] "So he said to him, 'You will be over five towns.'

[20] "And another came and said, 'Master, here is your mina. I have kept it hidden away in a cloth [21] because I was afraid of you, for you're a tough man: you collect what you didn't deposit and reap what you didn't sow.'

[22] "He told him, 'I will judge you by what you have said, you evil slave! If you knew I was a tough man, collecting what I didn't deposit and reaping what I didn't sow, [23] why didn't you put my

money in the bank? And when I returned, I would have collected it with interest!' ²⁴ So he said to those standing there, 'Take the mina away from him and give it to the one who has ten minas.'

²⁵ "But they said to him, 'Master, he has ten minas.'

²⁶ " 'I tell you, that to everyone who has, more will be given; and from the one who does not have, even what he does have will be taken away. ²⁷ But bring here these enemies of mine, who did not want me to rule over them, and slaughter them in my presence.' "

THE TRIUMPHAL ENTRY

²⁸ When He had said these things, He went on ahead, going up to Jerusalem. ²⁹ As He approached Bethphage and Bethany, at the place called the Mount of Olives, He sent two of the disciples ³⁰ and said, "Go into the village ahead of you. As you enter it, you will find a young donkey tied there, on which no one has ever sat. Untie it and bring it here. ³¹ And if anyone asks you, 'Why are you untying it?' say this: 'The Lord needs it.' "

³² So those who were sent left and found it just as He had told them. ³³ As they were untying the young donkey, its owners said to them, "Why are you untying the donkey?"

³⁴ "The Lord needs it," they said. ³⁵ Then they brought it to Jesus, and after throwing their robes on the donkey, they helped Jesus get on it. ³⁶ As He was going along, they were spreading their robes on the road. ³⁷ Now He came near the path down the Mount of Olives, and the whole crowd of the disciples began to praise God joyfully with a loud voice for all the miracles they had seen:

³⁸ "Blessed is the King who comes in the name of the Lord.

Peace in heaven and glory in the highest heaven!"

³⁹ And some of the Pharisees from the crowd told Him, "Teacher, rebuke Your disciples."

⁴⁰ He answered, "I tell you, if they were to keep silent, the stones would cry out!"

JESUS' LOVE FOR JERUSALEM

⁴¹ As He approached and saw the city, He wept over it, saying, "If you knew this day what leads to peace—but now it is hidden from your eyes. ⁴³ For the days will come upon you when your enemies will build an embankment against you, surround you and hem you in on every side. ⁴⁴ They will crush you and your children within you to the ground, and they will not leave one stone on another in you, because you did not recognize the time of your visitation."

CLEANSING THE TEMPLE COMPLEX

⁴⁵ He went into the temple complex and began to throw out those who were selling, ⁴⁶ and He said, "It is written, 'My house will be a house of prayer,' but you have made it 'a den of thieves!'"

⁴⁷ Every day He was teaching in the temple complex. The chief priests, the scribes, and the leaders of the people were looking for a way to destroy Him, ⁴⁸ but they could not find a way to do it, because all the people were spellbound by what they heard.

Christ Cleansing the Temple

The worship of God and human enterprise often pass close. Adoration and personal profit are easy to confuse. When Jesus took a flog and ran through the temple driving the holy profiteers before him, he was trying to say, come to the worship of God for the right reasons.

Find that temple where God lives and bend your knee. Turn your eyes toward the throne and ask the psalmist's question. What are human beings that you are mindful of them? Then cleanse your life. Drive out those evil desires of self-service. Cleanse the temple of your heart. Let no motive live there which will not honor Christ.

There is no temple so inward or so holy as the heart in love with God.

Giordano (1632-1705) painted extremely decorative frescoes that in many ways influenced the Rococo style. Notice in this painting the tension between the violence of the scene and the look on Jesus' face — a simultaneous picture of divine love and wrath.

Then the Pharisees went and plotted how to trap Him by what He said. . . . But perceiving their malice, Jesus said, "Why are you testing Me, hypocrites?"

Rendering unto Caesar
MATTHEW 22:15, 18

Give the Pharisees one thing: They did their homework. They must have sat up well into the night in their cloistered meetings, twisting their beards, knitting their brows, shuffling the brittle pages of their wooden law in order to find something—*anything!*—that could shoot holes in the theology of this prophetic pretender.

Here's one for you, Jesus. Is it lawful to pay taxes to Caesar or not? (Let's see him wiggle out of this one.)

Jesus faced a theological cul-de-sac here. If he said, "Honor Rome," many Jews would erupt in anger against him. If he said, "Honor the Jewish state," the Romans would suspect him of treason. So he answered in that middle ground that honors both.

Rendering unto Caesar is in every way fair. Caesar provides the good things that come from corporate government. Still, within a generation after Jesus told his followers to take care of Caesar, Caesar had destroyed both Jews and Christians. When Caesar told them they could not worship the true God—when Caesar told them they must abandon Jesus as their Lord—then it became clear that at that point, under those terms, they must render unto God what was God's.

Two kingdoms, two citizenships: These are the provinces of all believers. We should honor our civil rulers, unless they tell us that Christ is to be abandoned or that we are no longer free to worship him as his Word requires. Then our first allegiance belongs to Christ. When Caesar tried to deny Christians their right to live and participate in the kingdom of God, then Christians had to declare their loyalty to the Savior. When the law books contradict the Christian's Book, we must remember that we are "a chosen race, a royal priesthood, a holy nation, His own people" (1 Pt 2:9).

This was not a matter of tax evasion for the man of Nazareth! Jesus paid his taxes, but his entire life belonged to another kingdom whose flag is a banner of the heart and whose requirements are stiffer than the most punitive tax code.

PRAYER
Lord, I want to live out my citizenship in this my home country, always rendering unto Caesar that which is his. But heighten my longing for that city to which I'm headed—that city built foursquare, whose builder and maker is God.

CHAPTER TWENTY-THREE

THE PARABLE OF THE WEDDING BANQUET

Once more Jesus spoke to them in parables: [2] "The kingdom of heaven may be compared to a king who gave a wedding banquet for his son. [3] He sent out his slaves to summon those invited to the banquet, but they didn't want to come. [4] Again, he sent out other slaves, and said, 'Tell those who are invited, "Look, I've prepared my dinner; my oxen and fatted cattle have been slaughtered, and everything is ready. Come to the wedding banquet."'

[5] "But they paid no attention and went away, one to his own farm, another to his business. [6] And the others seized his slaves and killed them. [7] The king was enraged, so he sent out his troops, destroyed those murderers, and burned down their city.

[8] "Then he told his slaves, 'The banquet is ready, but those who were invited were not worthy. [9] Therefore, go to where the roads exit the city and invite everyone you find to the banquet.' [10] So those

slaves went out on the roads and gathered everyone they found, both evil and good. The wedding banquet was filled with guests. [11] But when the king came in to view the guests, he saw a man there who was not dressed for a wedding. [12] So he said to him, 'Friend, how did you get in here without wedding clothes?' The man was speechless.

[13] "Then the king told the attendants, 'Tie him up hand and foot, and throw him into the outer darkness, where there will be weeping and gnashing of teeth.'

[14] "For many are invited, but few are chosen."

GOD AND CAESAR

[15] Then the Pharisees went and plotted how to trap Him by what He said. [16] They sent their disciples to Him, with the Herodians. "Teacher," they said, "we know that You are truthful and teach the way of God in truth. You defer to no one, for You don't show partiality. [17] Tell us, therefore, what You think. Is it lawful to pay taxes to Caesar or not?"

[18] But perceiving their malice, Jesus said, "Why are you testing Me, hypocrites? [19] Show Me the coin used for the tax." So they brought Him a denarius. [20] "Whose image and inscription is this?" He asked them.

[21] "Caesar's," they said to Him.

Then He said to them, "Therefore, give back to Caesar the things that are Caesar's, and to God the things that are God's."

²² When they heard this, they were amazed. So they left Him and went away.

THE SADDUCEES AND THE RESURRECTION

²³ The same day some Sadducees, who say there is no resurrection, came up to Him and questioned Him: ²⁴ "Teacher, Moses said, 'if a man dies, having no children, his brother is to marry his wife and raise up offspring for his brother.' ²⁵ Now there were seven brothers among us. The first got married and died. Having no offspring, he left his wife to his brother. ²⁶ The same happened to the second also, and the third, and so to all seven. ²⁷ Then last of all the woman died. ²⁸ Therefore, in the resurrection, whose wife will she be of the seven? For they all had married her."

²⁹ Jesus answered them, "You are deceived, because you don't know the Scriptures or the power of God. ³⁰ For in the resurrection they neither marry nor are given in marriage, but are like angels in heaven. ³¹ Now concerning the resurrection of the dead, haven't you read what was spoken to you by God: ³² 'I am the God of Abraham and the God of Isaac and the God of Jacob'? He is not the God of the dead, but of the living."

³³ And when the crowds heard this, they were astonished at His teaching.

THE PRIMARY COMMANDMENTS

[34] When the Pharisees heard that He had silenced the Sadducees, they came together in the same place. [35] And one of them, an expert in the law, asked a question to test Him: [36] "Teacher, which commandment in the law is the greatest?"

[37] He said to him, " 'You shall love the Lord your God with all your heart, with all your soul, and with all your mind.' [38] This is the greatest and most important commandment. [39] The second is like it: 'You shall love your neighbor as yourself.' [40] All the Law and the Prophets depend on these two commandments."

THE QUESTION ABOUT THE MESSIAH

[41] While the Pharisees were together, Jesus questioned them, [42] "What do you think about the Messiah? Whose Son is He?"

"David's," they told Him.

[43] He asked them, "How is it then that David, inspired by the Spirit, calls Him 'Lord':

[44] The Lord said to my Lord,

'Sit at My right hand

Until I put Your enemies under Your feet'?

[45] "If, then, David calls Him 'Lord,' how is He his Son?" [46] No one was able to answer Him at all, and from that day no one dared to question Him any more.

The Raising of Lazarus

To see clearly the outcome of the cross, we must first allow the purple shadows of Good Friday to steal hope, purpose, and meaning form everything that Jesus ever claimed. Then we must see the gray dawn of the middle day, when the Son of God, reduced to a human corpse, lay silent in the grave. Here was despair that could find no resolution. To every eye it appeared that he was dead—forever dead! Wrapped in silent parables and soundless songs, he who claimed to be "the life" was dead. The mists of that middle day blurred eyes with grief and gripped the hearts of believers with the painful consciousness that they had given him their allegiance in vain. So the weary weekend was over. And it was just at the place where the long, long second day faded into the next that God wrote a victorious epilogue to Friday's defeat.

The cross was God's finest effort to demonstrate his love, but we would never have stopped to consider it without the resurrection. And, without the majesty and sacrifice of the cross, we would have forgotten the resurrection in a fortnight. The resurrection is as historical as the cross, and they are both imperative to our faith.

By Calvin Miller, From *Once upon a Tree*, Baker Book House

Fabritius (1622-1654), a Dutch painter who studied under Rembrandt, reflects his master's style in this piece which, though not exactly in harmony with the Gospel account, places the light source inside the tomb to show new life dispelling the darkness of the grave.

Jesus said to him, "You see these great buildings? Not one stone will be left here on another that will not be thrown down!". . . "Tell us, when will these things happen? And what will be the sign when all these things are about to take place?"

When Cultures Crumble

MARK 13:2, 4

Nothing is permanent. That was Jesus' message for disciples marveling over the great architectural wonder of the temple. It was hard for the disciples to believe that anything—whether a natural catastrophe or post-war dismantling—would ever destroy the colossal buildings of the temple. Jesus reminded them that their euphoria was unreasonable. The buildings would come down. Like their own times, all buildings are impermanent. A day was coming when not even one stone of the temple would be left upon another.

Naturally, after such a downsizing of their moods, the disciples' next question was "when?" "When" is a very human question. Our lives are so short that we are continually preoccupied with clocks or, as in the case of the disciples, sundials. Sand, like our lives, is always running through the constriction of the hourglass.

In a later day when Peter wrote his second letter, many people were saying, "Where is the promise of His coming? For ever since the fathers fell asleep everything continues as it has been since the beginning of creation" (2 Pt 3:4). Peter replied, "But do not be unaware of this one thing, dear friends: that with the Lord one day is like 1,000 years, and 1,000 years like one day" (2 Pt 3:8).

"When" is too much a matter of the clock for us, as we inquire of God about the end of the world. Having only seventy years or so of life, we strain to see God move history fast enough for us to measure and date it all. God is in no such hurry. With him a thousand years are but a day. So, take a load off your impatient minds. Jesus is, indeed, on the way back, but the date of his coming is left entirely to the keeping of the casual God and not the neurotic, clock-driven masses.

So what shall we do till he comes? We shall break the bread and drink the wine and remember that he who comes the second time bought us by bleeding when he came the first time.

PRAYER

Lord, help me to watch without becoming neurotic. My job is to serve you and attend to the why of my life, while you attend to all the whens, including that wonderful face-to-face moment of your return.

CHAPTER TWENTY-FOUR

FROM THE GOSPEL OF MARK, CHAPTER 13

DESTRUCTION OF THE TEMPLE PREDICTED

As He was going out of the temple complex, one of His disciples said to Him, "Teacher, look! What massive stones! What impressive buildings!"

² Jesus said to him, "You see these great buildings? Not one stone will be left here on another that will not be thrown down!"

SIGNS OF THE END OF THE AGE

³ While He was sitting on the Mount of Olives across from the temple complex, Peter, James, John, and Andrew asked Him privately, ⁴ "Tell us, when will these things happen? And what will be the sign when all these things are about to take place?"

⁵ Then Jesus began by telling them: "Watch out that no one deceives you. ⁶ Many will come in My

name, saying, 'I am He,' and they will deceive many. [7] When you hear of wars and rumors of wars, don't be alarmed; these things must take place, but the end is not yet. [8] For nation will rise up against nation, and kingdom against kingdom. There will be earthquakes in various places, and famines. These are the beginning of birth pains.

PERSECUTIONS PREDICTED

[9] "But you, be on your guard! They will hand you over to sanhedrins, and you will be flogged in the synagogues. You will stand before governors and kings because of Me, as a witness to them. [10] And the good news must first be proclaimed to all nations. [11] So when they arrest you and hand you over, don't worry beforehand what you will say. On the contrary, whatever is given to you in that hour—say it. For it isn't you who are speaking, but the Holy Spirit. [12] Then brother will betray brother to death, and a father his child. Children will rise up against parents and put them to death. [13] And you will be hated by all because of My name. But the one who endures to the end, this one will be delivered.

THE GREAT TRIBULATION

[14] "When you see the 'abomination that causes desolation' standing where it should not," (let the reader understand,) "then those in Judea must flee to the mountains! [15] A man on the housetop must not come down, or go in to get anything out of his house.

¹⁶ And a man in the field must not go back to get his clothes. ¹⁷ Woe to pregnant women and nursing mothers in those days! ¹⁸ Pray that it may not be in winter. ¹⁹ For those days will be a tribulation, the kind that hasn't been since the beginning of the world, which God created, until now, and never will be again! ²⁰ Unless the Lord cut short those days, no one would survive. But because of the elect, whom He chose, He cut short those days.

²¹ "Then if anyone tells you, 'Look, here is the Messiah! Look—there!' do not believe it! ²² For false messiahs and false prophets will rise up and will perform signs and wonders to lead astray, if possible, the elect. ²³ And you must watch! I have told you everything in advance.

THE COMING OF THE SON OF MAN

²⁴ "But in those days, after that tribulation,

> The sun will be darkened,
> and the moon will not shed her light;
> ²⁵ the stars will be falling from the sky,
> and the celestial powers will be shaken.

²⁶ Then they will see the Son of Man coming in clouds with great power and glory. ²⁷ Then He will send out the angels and gather His elect from the four winds, from the end of the earth to the end of the sky.

THE PARABLE OF THE FIG TREE

28 "Learn this parable from the fig tree: As soon as its branch becomes tender and sprouts leaves, you know that summer is near. 29 In the same way, when you see these things happening, know that He is near—at the door! 30 I assure you: This generation will certainly not pass away until all these things take place. 31 Heaven and earth will pass away, but My words will never pass away.

NO ONE KNOWS THE DAY OR HOUR

32 "Now concerning that day or hour no one knows—neither the angels in heaven, nor the Son—except the Father. 33 Watch! Be alert! For you don't know when the time is coming. 34 It is like a man on a journey, who left his house, gave authority to his slaves, gave each one his work, and commanded the doorkeeper to be alert. 35 Therefore be alert, since you don't know when the master of the house is coming—whether in the evening, or at midnight, or at the crowing of the rooster, or early in the morning. 36 Otherwise, he might come suddenly and find you sleeping. 37 And what I say to you, I say to everyone: Be alert!"

Jesus Washing Peter's Feet

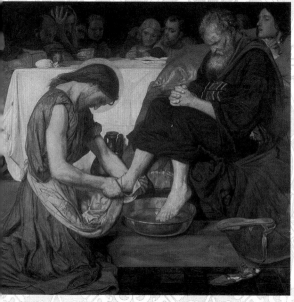

Once heaven wore a towel about her waist.
Once God knelt with a Basin
Once Majesty defined forever her wondrous condescension
Once did El-Shaddai genuflect
Before a fisherman and washed his feet.
Once angels wondered why.
Then the stooping Christ replied,
"If I wash not your feet you have no part of me."
Gladly then did universal pride confess itself.
For the servant is not greater than his Lord.

By Calvin Miller, From *My Journal*

Ford Maddox Brown (1821-1893) was an English Realist painter whose attention to detail resulted in canvasses almost photographic in quality. Witness Peter's prayerful pose, the disciple at the left reluctantly removing his sandals, and Judas grasping his head in guilt.

"Lord," said Philip, "show us the Father, and that's enough for us." Jesus said to him, "Have I been among you all this time without your knowing Me, Philip? The one who has seen Me has seen the Father. How can you say, 'Show us the Father'?

The Snapshot of God
JOHN 14:8-9

The face in Jesus' mirror was God! Philip's demand seems rather childish in many ways. Which child has not wanted to draw a picture of God? Yet children do not think it odd. Why do they want to draw a picture of God? Why did Philip want Jesus to do it? Because our finite hearts are always seeking to make mysteries declare themselves. We are so visually driven that we have convinced ourselves that what can't be seen doesn't exist. So Philip wanted a picture of God.

Jesus gave him one: himself. "Have I been so long with you, and you still don't know me? Would you see God, Philip? Then look at me. Here I am, Philip: I am God made visible in the only way that God will ever be seen. What I do, God does. What I say, God speaks. Have I been among you all this time without your knowing Me, Philip?"

Was Philip happy? Probably not for long. All of us shall always live feeling a little cheated. We want to see God, totally unaware that such a vision would blind us with its strong light. God's great reality is too grand for the sensate. Mystery—the mystery of godliness—is by its nature too large for our minds.

We must never forget that those things we can have pictures of—our houses, cars, our earthly bodies, the earth itself—are all in the act of passing away. The only enduring things are things nobody has pictures of—the Christ, heaven, the throne of God, the gilded vault of eternity.

Philip had to learn that the greatest truths are like butterflies: Try to pin them down, and you kill them. The best truth is unkillable, unpinnable, enduring. You have seen God when you have seen Jesus. That's why Jesus came—so that no one ever again would be able to say, "God is unknowable" or "God is invisible." God became Christ so that our eyes could see and our hands could handle the word of life.

PRAYER
Lord, you are the express image of the invisible God, even his eternal power and Godhead. I have seen you. I know exactly what God looks like. And that is enough for me.

CHAPTER TWENTY-FIVE

FROM THE GOSPEL OF JOHN, CHAPTER 14

THE WAY TO THE FATHER

"Your heart must not be troubled. Believe in God; believe also in Me. 2 In My Father's house are many dwelling places; if not, I would have told you. I am going away to prepare a place for you. 3 If I go away and prepare a place for you, I will come back and receive you to Myself, so that where I am you may be also. 4 You know the way where I am going."

5 "Lord," Thomas said, "we don't know where You're going. How can we know the way?"

6 Jesus told him, "I am the way, the truth, and the life. No one comes to the Father except through Me.

JESUS REVEALS THE FATHER

7 "If you know Me, you will also know My Father. From now on you do know Him and have seen Him."

8 "Lord," said Philip, "show us the Father, and that's enough for us."

9 Jesus said to him, "Have I been among you all this time without your knowing Me, Philip? The one who has seen Me has seen the Father. How can you say,

155

'Show us the Father'? [10] Don't you believe that I am in the Father and the Father is in Me? The words I speak to you I do not speak on My own. The Father who lives in Me does His works. [11] Believe Me that I am in the Father and the Father is in Me. Otherwise, believe because of the works themselves.

PRAYING IN JESUS' NAME

[12] "I assure you: The one who believes in Me will also do the works that I do. And he will do even greater works than these, because I am going to the Father. [13] Whatever you ask in My name, I will do it, so that the Father may be glorified in the Son. [14] If you ask Me anything in My name, I will do it.

ANOTHER COUNSELOR PROMISED

[15] "If you love Me, you will keep My commandments; [16] and I also will ask the Father, and He will give you another Counselor to be with you forever. [17] He is the Spirit of truth, whom the world is unable to receive because it doesn't see Him or know Him. But you do know Him, because He remains with you and will be in you. [18] I will not leave you as orphans; I am coming to you.

THE FATHER, THE SON, AND THE HOLY SPIRIT

[19] "In a little while the world will see Me no longer, but you will see Me. Because I live, you will live too. [20] In that day you will know that I am in My Father, you are in Me, and I am in you. [21] The one who has My commandments and keeps them is the one

who loves Me. And the one who loves Me will be loved by My Father. I also will love him and will reveal Myself to him."

²² Judas (not Iscariot) said to him, "Lord, how is it You're going to reveal Yourself to us and not to the world?"

²³ Jesus answered, "If anyone loves Me, he will keep My word. My Father will love him, and We will come to him and make Our home with him. ²⁴ The one who doesn't love Me will not keep My words. The word that you hear is not Mine, but is from the Father who sent Me.

²⁵ "I have spoken these things to you while I remain with you. ²⁶ But the Counselor, the Holy Spirit, whom the Father will send in My name, will teach you all things and remind you of everything I have told you.

JESUS' GIFT OF PEACE

²⁷ "Peace I leave with you. My peace I give to you. I do not give to you as the world gives. Your heart must not be troubled or fearful. ²⁸ You have heard me tell you, 'I am going away and I am coming to you.' If you loved Me, you would have rejoiced that I am going to the Father, because the Father is greater than I. ²⁹ I have told you now before it happens, so that when it does happen you may believe. ³⁰ I will not talk with you much longer, because the ruler of the world is coming. He has no power over Me. ³¹ On the contrary, I am going away so that the world may know that I love the Father. Just as the Father commanded Me, so I do.

"Get up; let's leave this place."

"I am the vine; you are the branches. The one who remains in Me and I in him produces much fruit, because you can do nothing without Me."

Abiding in the Vine
JOHN 15:5

Restless branch! Only two things curse the Christian's life. First, it may dry up for lack of nourishment. Second, it may curse itself with nonproductivity. Both of these curses are the result of an errant will. Do you will to be connected with the Vine? *The* Vine? Yes! The Vine is Christ. All things that matter in this world are connected with the Vine. There is no success without the Vine. There is no real wealth without the Vine. Would you be nourished and have the vitality that nourishment provides you? Then treasure your attachment to the Vine.

It seems such a simple piece of advice that Jesus gave us. In all the world of plants, what branch has managed to stay alive without being attached to the plant? Vines are meant to grow grapes. When they produce nothing, they frustrate the purpose of the vine. Then comes the pruning knife. It cuts. The vine bleeds and remembers its true nature. Jesus has to remind us of that which is so elementary: To live and flourish, we must be attached to Jesus. To mature in the spirit is a matter of this attachment.

How weakly many Christians live. They rarely stop and talk to Christ. They never read from his teachings. They make no effort to follow his example. They give no outer indications that they feel even a small amount of love for Christ. In short, they are unattached. They have mistaken busyness for life. They run after a hassled set of preoccupations. Their busy schedules make them think they are really happy and achieving. Yet there is nothing of value—no business or agenda—that exists when we are detached from the Vine.

Perhaps the best way of defining this metaphor is not vine attachment but one-ness with Christ. How much our littleness grows when we attach ourselves to his greatness. What significance we acquire when we attach ourselves to his eternal significance.

PRAYER
Lord, some days I find myself overly fatigued. Often I find myself somewhat depressed. Sometimes I feel like I'm struggling with unsolvable problems. The answer to all these things is the same: I am not attached to the nourishing of Christ. Forgive, dear Lord, this self-willed branch and help it to remember the secret of the overcoming life.

CHAPTER TWENTY-SIX

THE VINE AND THE BRANCHES

"I am the true vine, and My Father is the vineyard keeper. [2] Every branch in Me that does not produce fruit He removes, and He prunes every branch that produces fruit so that it will produce more fruit. [3] You are already clean because of the word I have spoken to you. [4] Remain in Me, and I in you. Just as a branch is unable to produce fruit by itself unless it remains on the vine, so neither can you unless you remain in Me.

[5] "I am the vine; you are the branches. The one who remains in Me and I in him produces much fruit, because you can do nothing without Me. [6] If anyone does not remain in Me, he is thrown aside like a branch and he withers. They gather them, throw them into the fire, and they are burned. [7] If you remain in Me and My words remain in you, ask whatever you want and it will be done for you. [8] My Father is glorified by this: that you produce much fruit and prove to be My disciples.

CHRISTLIKE LOVE

[9] "Just as the Father has loved Me, I also have loved you. Remain in My love. [10] If you keep My commandments you will remain in My love, just as I have kept My Father's commandments and remain in His love.

[11] "I have spoken these things to you so that My joy may be in you and your joy may be complete. [12] This is My commandment: that you love one another just as I have loved you. [13] No one has greater love than this, that someone would lay down his life for his friends. [14] You are My friends, if you do what I command you. [15] I do not call you slaves anymore, because a slave doesn't know what his master is doing. I have called you friends, because I have made known to you everything I have heard from My Father. [16] You did not choose Me, but I chose you. I appointed you that you should go out and produce fruit, and that your fruit should remain, so that whatever you ask the Father in My name, He will give you. [17] This is what I command you: that you love one another.

PERSECUTIONS PREDICTED

[18] "If the world hates you, understand that it hated Me before it hated you. [19] If you were of the world, the world would love you as its own. However, because you are not of the world, but I have chosen you out of the world, this is why the world hates you. [20] Remember the word I spoke to you: 'A slave is not greater than his master.' If they persecuted Me, they will also persecute you. If they kept My word, they will also keep yours. [21] But they will do all these things to you on account of My name, because they don't know the One who sent Me. [22] If I had not come and spoken to

them, they would not have sin. Now they have no excuse for their sin. [23] The one who hates Me also hates My Father. [24] If I had not done the works among them that no one else has done, they would not have sin. Now they have seen and hated both Me and My Father. [25] But this happened so that the statement written in their law might be fulfilled: 'They hated me for no reason.'

COMING TESTIMONY AND REJECTION

[26] "When the Counselor comes, whom I will send to you from the Father—the Spirit of truth who proceeds from the Father—He will testify about Me. [27] You also will testify, because you have been with Me from the beginning."

"When the Spirit of truth comes, He will guide you into all the truth. For He will not speak on His own, but He will speak whatever He hears. He will also declare to you what is to come. He will glorify Me, because He will take from what is Mine and declare it to you."

The Glorifying Spirit
JOHN 16:13-14

The Holy Spirit's threefold role is to guide, glorify, and disclose. His guidance helps us find our way. His glorification is our worship. His disclosure reveals the next step in our pilgrimage of love. Consider the glory of his threefold role:

His guidance, like the North Star, is the focus for our navigation through rough seas. Other stars may waste themselves in forming old Greek constellations, but Polaris guides. Direction is his gift. Guidance is his currency when you cannot find your way. His guidance says that tomorrow will be accessible, at least by sunrise. He is there, and the light for your future may not shine far, but it will illuminate your next step.

His glorification is that praise that you give him. What does that praise do? It is so centered on his magnificence that as you glorify him, your heart will lose its grip on those little miseries that keep you apart from him. Glorification is never achieved by making yourself smaller but by enlarging his sovereignty over your small affairs every day.

His disclosure lets you see what lies behind that heavy veil called tomorrow. Disclosure is but another word for revelation. What you cannot see makes you afraid, and so God draws the drapes to show you the future. Disclosure is the source of pure joy! It is the delight of your heavenly Father to unwrap your future, to uncase his plans, to take the manna of your survival out of hiddenness. Then you will know what you need to know to live in your world. We see what we had never seen before, and the sight is glorious. Do we see everything? All of the will of God, for our lives, for all time? All of it? No. But enough of it that we can see the next step we can take in safety.

So blessed Spirit of God, guide me; the night is somehow too dark to see without you. Glorify the Son through my life. Let my tongue sing his praises until all my self-absorption is lost. Disclose these truths that shatter all my dull routines with wonder.

PRAYER
Lord, I own my way when you guide. I worship when I glorify you. I see as you disclose. So please guide, glorify, and disclose from the center of my life.

CHAPTER TWENTY-SEVEN

"I have told you these things to keep you from stumbling. ² They will ban you from the synagogues. In fact, a time is coming when anyone who kills you will think he is offering service to God. ³ They will do these things because they haven't known the Father or Me. ⁴ But I have told you these things so that when their time comes you may remember I told them to you. I didn't tell you these things from the beginning, because I was with you.

THE COUNSELOR'S MINISTRY

⁵ "But now I am going away to Him who sent Me, and not one of you asks Me, 'Where are you going?' ⁶ Yet, because I have spoken these things to you, sorrow has filled your heart. ⁷ Nevertheless, I am telling you the truth. It is for your benefit that I go away, because if I don't go away the Counselor will not come to you. If I go, I will send Him to you. ⁸ When He comes, He will convict the world about sin, righteousness, and judgment: ⁹ about sin, because they do not believe in Me;

[10] about righteousness, because I am going to the Father and you will no longer see Me; [11] and about judgment, because the ruler of this world has been judged.

[12] "I still have many things to tell you, but you can't bear them now. [13] When the Spirit of truth comes, He will guide you into all the truth. For He will not speak on His own, but He will speak whatever He hears. He will also declare to you what is to come. [14] He will glorify Me, because He will take from what is Mine and declare it to you. [15] Everything the Father has is Mine. This is why I told you that He takes from what is Mine and will declare it to you.

SORROW TURNED TO JOY

[16] "A little while and you will no longer see Me; again a little while and you will see Me."

[17] Therefore some of His disciples said to one another, "What is this He tells us: 'A little while and you will not see Me; again a little while and you will see Me'; and, 'because I am going to the Father'?" [18] They said, "What is this He is saying, 'A little while'? We don't know what He's talking about!"

[19] Jesus knew they wanted to question Him, so He said to them, "Are you asking one another about what I said, 'A little while and you will not see Me; again a little while and you will see Me'?

[20] "I assure you: You will weep and wail, but the world will rejoice. You will become sorrowful, but your sorrow will turn to joy. [21] When a woman is in labor she has pain because her time has come. But when she has given birth to a child, she no longer remembers the

suffering because of the joy that a person has been born into the world. 22 So you also have sorrow now. But I will see you again. Your hearts will rejoice, and no one will rob you of your joy. 23 In that day you will not ask Me anything.

"I assure you: Anything you ask the Father in My name, He will give you. 24 Until now you have asked for nothing in My name. Ask and you will receive, that your joy may be complete.

JESUS THE VICTOR

25 "I have spoken these things to you in figures of speech. A time is coming when I will no longer speak to you in figures, but I will tell you plainly about the Father. 26 In that day you will ask in My name. I am not telling you that I will make requests to the Father on your behalf. 27 For the Father Himself loves you, because you have loved Me and have believed that I came from God. 28 I came from the Father and have come into the world. Again, I am leaving the world and going to the Father."

29 "Ah!" His disciples said. "Now You're speaking plainly and not using any figurative language. 30 Now we know that You know everything and don't need anyone to question You. By this we believe that You came from God."

31 Jesus responded to them, "Do you now believe? 32 Look: An hour is coming, and has come, when you will be scattered each to his own home, and you will leave Me alone. Yet I am not alone, because the Father is with Me. 33 I have told you these things so that in Me you may have peace. In the world you have suffering. But take courage! I have conquered the world."

"I have glorified You on the earth by completing the work You gave Me to do.

The Promise Keepers
JOHN 17:4

Jesus celebrated the victory before the decisive battle. He gloried in all that he would shortly finish—all that God had called him to do. The dying still lay ahead of him, but the purpose for his living on earth in time was all finished. Knowing that we shall complete the tasks God gives us to finish is that inner reward that makes our time to die a time of celebration.

The apostle Paul experienced an interesting metamorphosis in his view of death. In 1 Thessalonians he seems to believe that he will not die, but will see the coming of the Lord in his own lifetime. He encouraged the Thessalonians to remember that those who had already died before Jesus returned would be the first to be raised in the Second Coming. Then referring to his own future expectation, he continued, "For we say this to you by the word of the Lord: that we who are alive and are left until the coming of the Lord will not go ahead of those who have fallen asleep" (1 Th 4:15).

But consider his view in 2 Timothy, written at a much later date: "For I am already being poured out as a drink offering, and the time for my departure has come. I have fought the good fight; I have finished the course; I have kept the faith" (2 Tm 4:6,7). Having finished the race is Paul's way of saying what Jesus said: "I have completed the work you gave Me to do."

The great burden of every follower of Christ is to come to know what God has called us to do in this world. Once we know this, we will have that unspeakable joy of anticipating how we will feel when we have done it. Dying knows a double blessing. The first blessing comes in possessing the security that when we close our eyes in death we will open them in heaven. The second blessing is the knowledge of having lived out our calling. Then we may give our lives to completing the task he gave us to do.

PRAYER
Lord, I thank you for the gifts of the Spirit. It is your blessed Holy Spirit that has taught me my calling. Now that I am in the world, for as long as I am in the world, I will seek to complete all that you have given me to do. How glorious must be your final "well done" to those who knew what you wanted done and never lacked direction or purpose in their living.

CHAPTER TWENTY-EIGHT

FROM THE GOSPEL OF JOHN, CHAPTER 17

JESUS PRAYS FOR HIMSELF

Jesus spoke these things, then raised His eyes to heaven, and said:

> "Father, the hour has come.
> Glorify Your Son so that the Son may glorify You,
> ² just as You gave Him authority over all flesh;
> so that He may give eternal life to all You have given Him.
> ³ This is eternal life: that they may know You, the only true God,
> and the One You have sent—Jesus Christ.
> ⁴ I have glorified You on the earth
> by completing the work You gave Me to do.
> ⁵ Now, Father, glorify Me in Your presence

with that glory I had with You before the world
existed.

JESUS PRAYS FOR HIS DISCIPLES

6 "I have revealed Your name to the men You gave Me
from the world.
They were Yours, You gave them to Me,
and they have kept Your word.

7 Now they know that all things You have given to
Me are from You,

8 because the words that You gave to Me, I have given
to them.
They have received them and have known for
certain
that I came from You.
They have believed that You sent Me.

9 I pray for them. I am not praying for the world,
but for those You have given Me,
because they are Yours.

10 All My things are Yours, and Yours are Mine,
and I have been glorified in them.

11 I am no longer in the world, but they are in the
world, and I am coming to You.
Holy Father, protect them by Your name
that You have given Me,
so that they may be one just as We are.

¹² While I was with them I was protecting them

by Your name that You have given me.

I guarded them and not one of them is lost, except

the son of destruction, that the Scripture may be

fulfilled.

¹³ Now I am coming to You, and I speak these things

in the world so that they may have My joy

completed in them.

¹⁴ I have given them Your word.

The world hated them because they are not of

the world, just as I am not of the world.

¹⁵ I am not praying that You take them out of the

world, but that You protect them from the evil one.

¹⁶ They are not of the world, just as I am not of the

world.

¹⁷ Sanctify them by the truth; Your word is truth.

¹⁸ Just as You sent Me into the world,

I also have sent them into the world.

¹⁹ I sanctify Myself for them,

so they also may be sanctified by the truth.

JESUS PRAYS FOR ALL BELIEVERS

²⁰ "I pray not only for these, but also for those

who believe in Me through their message.

²¹ May they all be one, just as You, Father,

are in Me and I am in You.

May they also be one in Us,

so that the world may believe You sent Me.

²² I have given them the glory that You have given to
Me.

May they be one just as We are one.

²³ I am in them and You are in Me.

May they be made completely one,

so that the world may know You sent Me

and that You have loved them just as You have
loved Me,

²⁴ Father, I desire those You have given Me to be with
Me where I am.

Then they may see My glory, which You have
given Me, because You loved Me before the
world's foundation.

²⁵ Righteous Father! The world has not known You.
However, I have known You,

and these have known that You sent Me.

²⁶ I made Your name known to them and will make
it known,so that the love with which You have
loved Me may be in them,

and that I may be in them."

The Last Supper

A young rabbi, followed by a dozen husky men once sat down at a massive table, and a flagon of wine was emptied into a single cup. Each of the men had anticipated Thursday's party as a time of levity and warmth, but when the hour had come, there was an unspoken dread in the air that choked lightheartedness. It seemed to be such an ordinary Thursday and, beyond it, only and ordinary Friday. But nothing was ordinary. A ghastly picture of Friday lay unseen on the surface of Thursday's wine. Ominously the portent floated on the deep-red liquid, framed by the oval rim of the metal chalice. What was the omen that lay unnoticed on the crimson-purple surface of the wine? It was a man with a hammer.

As he lifted the cup he said to them, "Do this in remembrance of Me" (1 Co 11:24). In effect, he was saying, "Remember tomorrow! For what shall happen tomorrow concerns everyone who ever shall live. God shall have nails in his hands tomorrow. Tomorrow, I shall die. Remember tomorrow."

Dramatically Jesus reached for Thursday's loaf. With almost sudden violence, he tore it in two and said what seemed to say, "Do you see this bread? Eat it! Tomorrow my body will be torn like this!" Then he breathed a prayer and lifted the cup and spoke the phrase whose larger meaning was: "My blood will flow as easily as this wine. Drink it and remember tomorrow!".

Taken from *Once Upon A Tree* by Calvin Miller, pp. 89-92

Peter Paul Rubens depicts the Last Supper in a way that emphasizes the centrality of Christ and Peter, who is the first apostle to receive the bread and wine.

When those around Him saw what was going to happen, they asked, "Lord, should we strike with the sword?" Then one of them struck the high priest's slave and cut off his right ear. But Jesus responded, "No more of this!" And touching his ear, He healed him.

Without a Struggle
LUKE 22:49-51

Was Jesus a militant Messiah? One severed ear was the only casualty of his entire struggle to establish his kingdom; yet it was one ear too many. So it was that Jesus instantly healed this hacked-up servant. Perhaps this healing was Jesus' way of saying, "Not one ear, not one little bit of blood is to be shed in my kingdom of peace."

In the healing of this ear was born a noble idea. Jesus gave birth to it when he said that we are to learn to turn the other cheek. If anyone strikes us on one cheek, we are to offer him the other as well. Here was born the nonviolent principle that so many of this world's great social reformers would use later to tame hypocrisy and prejudice.

Think what a bloodbath would have followed if Jesus had encouraged the severing of ears. Would not the soldiers who came for his arrest have jousted with his groggy disciples? Would not a revolution of some sort have been born? Would not the peaceable kingdom have erupted in war? This was not to be the way of Jesus' kingdom.

Now the ear was healed. Now all the military conflict there would ever be was over. Now Jesus could remind them that they were to conquer the world by dying but never by killing. Now they would be able to see that here was a kingdom that would bring the mighty army of Rome to its knees without lifting a single sword.

So they began to die. Jesus was the first to do so. In the next three hundred years several hundred thousand more would taste death. Each time they died, the world lived a little more. Each time they perished for their faith, more came to believe. Until shortly after A.D. 300, the killings were over. Christianity had won the right to stand! All the overcoming of this great way of life began when Malchus lost an ear and Jesus said, "Put up your sword!" From that point on, Christianity became a bloodless revolution that would never know defeat because love never fails.

PRAYER
Lord, I am never in danger of killing anyone to prove my militant loyalty to you. Sometimes, Lord, I do find myself forgetting that most killing begins in the hearts of those who have been willing to hurt someone else. Help me to be so gentle of spirit that I would never cause pain to someone whom you are reaching to include in your kingdom of love.

CHAPTER TWENTY-NINE

THE PLOT TO KILL JESUS

The Festival of Unleavened Bread, which is called Passover, was drawing near. ² The chief priests and the scribes were looking for a way to put Him to death, because they were afraid of the people.

³ Then Satan entered Judas, called Iscariot, who was numbered among the Twelve. ⁴ He went away and discussed with the chief priests and temple police how he could hand Him over to them. ⁵ They were glad, and agreed to give him silver. ⁶ So he accepted the offer and started looking for a good opportunity to betray Him to them when the crowd was not present.

PREPARATION FOR PASSOVER

⁷ Then the Day of Unleavened Bread came, on which the Passover lamb had to be sacrificed. ⁸ Jesus sent Peter and John, saying, "Go and prepare the Passover meal for us, so we may eat it."

⁹ "Where do You want us to prepare it?" they asked Him.

¹⁰ "Listen," He said to them, "when you've entered the city, a man carrying a water jug will meet you. Follow him into the house that he enters. ¹¹ Tell the owner of the house, 'The Teacher asks you, "Where is the guest room, where I may eat the Passover with My disciples?" ' ¹² Then he will show you a large, furnished room upstairs. Make the preparations there."

¹³ So they went and found it just as He had told them, and they prepared the Passover.

THE FIRST LORD'S SUPPER

¹⁴ When the hour came, He reclined at the table, and the apostles with Him. ¹⁵ Then He said to them, "I have fervently desired to eat this Passover with you before I suffer. ¹⁶ For I tell you, I will not eat it again until it is fulfilled in the kingdom of God." ¹⁷ Then He took a cup, and after giving thanks, He said, "Take this and share it among yourselves. ¹⁸ For I tell you, from now on I will not drink of the fruit of the vine until the kingdom of God comes."

¹⁹ And He took bread, gave thanks, broke it, gave it to them, and said, "This is My body, which is given for you. Do this in remembrance of Me."

²⁰ In the same way He also took the cup after supper and said, "This cup is the new covenant in My blood, which is shed for you. ²¹ But look, the hand of the one betraying Me is at the table with Me! ²² For the Son of Man will go away as it has been determined, but woe to that man by whom He is betrayed!"

²³ So they began to argue among themselves which of them it could be who was going to do this thing.

THE DISPUTE OVER GREATNESS

²⁴ Then a dispute also arose among them about who should be considered the greatest. ²⁵ But He said to them, "The kings of the Gentiles dominate them, and those who have authority over them are called 'Benefactors.' ²⁶ But it must not be like that among you. On the contrary, whoever is greatest among you must become like the youngest, and whoever leads, like the one serving. ²⁷ For who is greater, the one at the table or the one serving? Isn't it the one at the table? But I am among you as the One who serves. ²⁸ You are the ones who stood by Me in My trials. ²⁹ I grant you a kingdom, just as My Father granted one to Me, ³⁰ so that you may eat and drink at My table in My kingdom. And you will sit on thrones judging the twelve tribes of Israel.

PETER'S DENIAL PREDICTED

³¹ "Simon, Simon, look out! Satan has asked to sift you like wheat. ³² But I have prayed for you, that your faith may not fail. And you, when you have turned back, strengthen your brothers."

³³ "Lord," he told Him, "I'm ready to go with You both to prison and to death!"

³⁴ "I tell you, Peter," He said, "the rooster will not crow today until you deny three times that you know Me!"

MONEY-BAG, BACKPACK, AND SWORD

[35] He also said to them, "When I sent you out without money-bag, backpack, or sandals, did you lack anything?"

"Not a thing," they said.

[36] Then He said to them, "But now whoever has a money-bag should take it, and also a backpack. And whoever doesn't have a sword should sell his robe and buy one. [37] For I tell you, what is written must be fulfilled in Me: 'And He was counted among the outlaws.' Yes, what is written about Me is coming to its fulfillment."

[38] "Lord," they said, "look, here are two swords."

"Enough of that!" He told them.

THE PRAYER IN THE GARDEN

[39] He went out and made His way as usual to the Mount of Olives, and the disciples also followed Him. [40] When He reached the place, He told them, "Pray that you may not enter into temptation." [41] Then He withdrew from them about a stone's throw, knelt down, and began to pray, [42] "Father, if You are willing, take this cup away from Me—nevertheless, not My will, but Yours, be done."

([43] Then an angel from heaven appeared to Him, strengthening Him. [44] Being in anguish, He prayed more fervently, and His sweat became like drops of blood falling to the ground.) [45] When He got up from prayer and came to the disciples, He found them sleeping, exhausted from their grief. [46] "Why are you sleeping?" He asked them. "Get up and pray, so that you may not enter into temptation."

THE JUDAS KISS

[47] While He was still speaking, suddenly a mob was there, and one of the Twelve named Judas was leading them. He came near Jesus to kiss Him, [48] but Jesus said to him, "Judas, are you betraying the Son of Man with a kiss?"

[49] When those around Him saw what was going to happen, they asked, "Lord, should we strike with the sword?" [50] Then one of them struck the high priest's slave and cut off his right ear.

[51] But Jesus responded, "No more of this!" And touching his ear, He healed him. [52] Then Jesus said to the chief priests, temple police, and the elders who had come for Him, "Have you come out with swords and clubs as if I were a criminal? [53] Every day while I was with you in the temple complex, you never laid a hand on Me. But this is your hour—and the dominion of darkness."

PETER DENIES HIS LORD

[54] They seized Him, led Him away, and brought Him into the high priest's house. Meanwhile Peter was following at a distance. [55] When they had lit a fire in the middle of the courtyard and sat down together, Peter sat among them. [56] When a servant saw him sitting in the firelight, and looked closely at him, she said, "This man was with Him too."

[57] But he denied it: "Woman, I don't know Him!"

[58] After a little while, someone else saw him and said, "You're one of them too!"

"Man, I am not!" Peter said.

⁵⁹ About an hour later, another kept insisting, "This man was certainly with Him, since he's also a Galilean."

⁶⁰ But Peter said, "Man, I don't know what you're talking about!" Immediately, while he was still speaking, a rooster crowed. ⁶¹ Then the Lord turned and looked at Peter. So Peter remembered the word of the Lord, how He had said to him, "Before the rooster crows today, you will deny Me three times." ⁶² And he went outside and wept bitterly.

JESUS MOCKED AND BEATEN

⁶³ The men who were holding Jesus started mocking and beating Him. ⁶⁴ After blindfolding Him, they kept asking, "Prophesy! Who hit You?" ⁶⁵ And they were saying many other blasphemous things against Him.

JESUS FACES THE SANHEDRIN

⁶⁶ When daylight came, the elders of the people, both the chief priests and the scribes, convened and brought Him before their Sanhedrin. ⁶⁷ They said, "If You are the Messiah, tell us."

But He said to them, "If I do tell you, you will not believe. ⁶⁸ And if I ask you, you will not answer. ⁶⁹ But from now on, the Son of Man will be seated at the right hand of the Power of God."

⁷⁰ They all asked, "Are You, then, the Son of God?"

And He said to them, "You say that I am."

⁷¹ "Why do we need any more testimony," they said, "since we've heard it ourselves from His mouth?"

Procession to Calvary

The crucifixion happened on a busy market day when many people were doubtless coming into the city to do their last-minute shopping for the Passover holidays. This was such an important Jewish holiday that the city was thronged with pilgrims returning to the Holy Land from every province of the Roman Empire. The cross had likely drawn an international crowd of onlookers. They were not completely disinterested, for they had stopped to watch. Yet they were not interested in becoming any more involved than this, either.

These watchers saw it all. They watched the condemned man being spiked. They saw the cross as it was jolted upright in its socket. They heard the dull thud it made when it fell into its hole. They saw Jesus try in vain to find a way to make his head comfortable against the rugged timber of the cross.

The last ravages of our own human existence involve our trying to be comfortable while we die. Even those who crucify themselves in self-surrender struggle to find some way to hang conveniently while the unyielding wood makes no place for them to cradle their heads.

By Calvin Miller, From *Once upon a Tree*, Baker Book House

Bazzi (1477-1549) here synthesizes the major styles of Renaissance painting, juxtaposing compassion and violence. See the clenched fists of Christ's tormentors on the left, with the open hands of the man at right and the compassion of Simon who stoops to help Him.

When it was noon, darkness came over the whole land until three in the afternoon. And at three Jesus cried out with a loud voice, "Eloi, Eloi, lemá sabachtháni?" which is translated, "My God, My God, why have You forsaken Me?"

The Ninth-Hour Cry
MARK 15:33-34

Christ's ordeal had stretched on hour after hour. He had been arrested, cuffed, beaten, stripped, mocked, and flogged. By this time his agony must have been at its apex. From this agony he cried out, "My God, My God, why have You forsaken Me?"

Let his agonizing cry seem as bold as it really was—the plaintive sobbing of a child who did not know how much more abuse he could withstand. See, too, the response of his Father. From heaven, his longing Father reached down toward his hurting son. Brokenness and pain caused the suffering Son to reach upward toward his Father. Thus, love united these broken lovers.

This cry from the cross illustrates the humanity of Christ, but so much more. If the human Jesus was hurting in the midst of all this pain, the divine Christ must have remembered all that being Christ Emmanuel meant.

This pain-wracked cry comes from the twenty-second psalm. In happier times, it had furnished Jesus with many wonderful moments of worship in the little synagogue at Nazareth. Then this psalm was only worship liturgy. On the cross it became a part of Jesus' dying appeal. What was once a song became a heart cry. When the cantor had sung it in the Nazarene synagogue, it was reflection. On the cross it became a throbbing and insistent question from God's broken Son: "Have you forsaken me?" Here is the issue of Jesus' anguish in a time of bleeding need.

If you must have an answer to this ninth-hour question, the answer is "No." God never forsook Jesus, just as Jesus never forsook his Father. God does hate sin. When Jesus bore the sins of the ages, God felt that remoteness that led him not to look on his Son; but he was with Jesus at every moment of his dying.

Best of all, here is Jesus' promise in your hard times. He will never leave you or forsake you. Is your own cross hard to bear? Is your dying an unspeakable agony? Go ahead and cry, *"Eloi, Eloi, lemá sabachtháni?"* God's answer to you is the same. It is always a resounding "No."

PRAYER
Lord, thanks for being there when life hurts. Just as you never forsook Jesus, I know you will not forsake me. Indeed, you cannot forsake me without making your Word a lie, and you are the God who cannot lie.

CHAPTER THIRTY

JESUS FACES PILATE

As soon as it was morning, the chief priests had a meeting with the elders, scribes and the whole Sanhedrin. After tying Jesus up, they led Him away and handed Him over to Pilate.

2 So Pilate asked Him, "Are You the King of the Jews?"

He answered him, "You have said it."

3 And the chief priests began to accuse Him of many things. 4 Then Pilate questioned Him again, "Are You not answering anything? Look how many things they are accusing You of!" 5 But Jesus still did not answer anything, so Pilate was amazed.

JESUS OR BARABBAS

6 At the festival it was Pilate's custom to release for them one prisoner whom they requested. 7 There was one named Barabbas, who was in prison with rebels who had committed murder in the rebellion. 8 The crowd came up and began to ask Pilate to do for them as was his custom. 9 So Pilate answered them, "Do you want me

to release the King of the Jews for you?" 10 For he knew it was because of envy that the chief priests had handed Him over. 11 But the chief priests stirred up the crowd so that he would release Barabbas to them instead.

12 Pilate asked them again, "Then what do you want me to do with the One you call the King of the Jews?"

13 And again they shouted, "Crucify Him!"

14 Then Pilate said to them, "Why? What has He done wrong?"

But they shouted, "Crucify Him!" all the more.

15 Then, willing to gratify the crowd, Pilate released Barabbas to them. And after having Jesus flogged, he handed Him over to be crucified.

MOCKED BY THE MILITARY

16 Then the soldiers led Him away into the courtyard (that is, headquarters) and called the whole company together. 17 They dressed Him in a purple robe, twisted a crown out of thorns, and put it on Him. 18 And they began to salute Him, "Hail, King of the Jews!" 19 They kept hitting Him on the head with a reed and spitting on Him. And getting down on their knees, they were paying Him homage. 20 When they had mocked Him, they stripped Him of the purple robe, put His clothes on Him, and led Him out to crucify Him.

CRUCIFIED BETWEEN TWO CRIMINALS

²¹ They forced a passer-by coming in from the country to carry His cross—Simon, a Cyrenian, the father of Alexander and Rufus. ²² And they brought Him to the place called Golgotha (which means Skull Place). ²³ They tried to give Him wine mixed with myrrh, but He did not take it. ²⁴ Then they crucified Him and divided His clothes, by casting lots for them, to decide what each would get. ²⁵ Now it was nine in the morning when they crucified Him. ²⁶ The inscription of the charge written against Him was:

THE KING OF THE JEWS

²⁷ They crucified two criminals with Him, one on the right and one on His left. (²⁸ So the Scripture was fulfilled that says: "And He was counted among outlaws.") ²⁹ Those who passed by were yelling insults at Him, shaking their heads and saying, "Ha! The One who would demolish the sanctuary and build it in three days, ³⁰ save Yourself by coming down from the cross!" ³¹ In the same way, the chief priests with the scribes, were mocking Him to one another and saying, "He saved others; He cannot save Himself! ³² Let the Messiah, the King of Israel, come down now from the cross, so that we may see and believe." Even those who were crucified with Him were taunting Him.

THE DEATH OF JESUS

³³ When it was noon, darkness came over the whole land until three in the afternoon. ³⁴ And at three Jesus cried out with a loud voice, *"Eloi, Eloi, lemá sabachtháni?"* which is translated, "My God, My God, why have You forsaken Me?"

[35] When some of those standing there heard this, they said, "Look, He's calling for Elijah!" [36] Someone ran and filled a sponge with sour wine, fixed it on a reed, offered Him a drink, and said, "Let us see if Elijah comes to take Him down!"

[37] But Jesus let out a loud cry and breathed His last. [38] Then the curtain of the sanctuary was split in two from top to bottom. [39] When the centurion, who was standing opposite Him, saw the way He breathed His last, he said, "This man really was God's Son!"

[40] There were also women looking on from a distance. Among them were Mary Magdalene, Mary the mother of James the younger and of Joses, and Salome. [41] When He was in Galilee, they would follow Him and minister to Him. Many other women had come up with Him to Jerusalem.

THE BURIAL OF JESUS

[42] When it was already evening, because it was Preparation Day (that is, the day before the Sabbath), [43] Joseph of Arimathea, a prominent member of the Sanhedrin who was himself looking forward to the kingdom of God, came and boldly went in to Pilate and asked for Jesus' body. [44] Pilate was surprised that He was already dead. Summoning the centurion, he asked him whether He had already died. [45] When he found out from the centurion, he granted the corpse to Joseph. [46] After he bought some fine linen, he took Him down and wrapped Him in the linen. Then he placed Him in a tomb cut out of the rock, and rolled a stone against the entrance to the tomb. [47] Now Mary Magdalene and Mary the mother of Joses were watching where He was placed.

The Crucifixion

The only reason the crucifixion came to be was that there were no alternatives. If there had been any other way for us to be saved, there would never have been a Calvary. Our Lord endured the ugliness of it all, not so we might have an alternate route of redemption, but because there was no other way. Had there been some less expensive way, the Son would never have gone back to the Father with scarred hands. Nor would he ever have suffered a naked death before his mother. The grieving God is our assurance that God died to answer our needs and our grief. So often our grief is our need. If there had been any other approach possible, the Lord would have shouted the command to angelic legions, waiting at rapt attention for the call to deliver him. The cross says emphatically, "Jesus is the Way—the only Way—the Truth, and the Life."

Peter Paul Rubens' artistic brilliance shines through in this gripping scene — from the agonized faces of the thieves, to the despairing faces of the women, to the almost emotionless faces of the soldiers as they inflict the final wound to the dead Christ.

Then He led them out as far as Bethany, and lifting up His hands He blessed them. And while He was blessing them, He left them and was carried up into heaven. After worshiping Him, they returned to Jerusalem with great joy.

The Never-Ending Story
LUKE 24:50-52

There is a double-exposure photograph in the heart of every believer. One image is of the dying Christ, captive to human laws and small decrees, crying, "It is finished!" The other image is of the Christ of the Apocalypse, bursting through the skies, clothed in lightning, crying, "History is finished!"

He is coming in the clouds with power and great glory. How wonderful it will be to behold this great finale! This is the great "not yet" of the New Testament. All else written there is now biblical history. Not this! Jesus, who left Olivet in A.D. 30 or so, has yet to complete that prophesy the two angelic men gave as Jesus rose into heaven. "Men of Galilee, why do you stand looking up into heaven? This Jesus, who has been taken from you into heaven, will come in the same way that you have seen Him going into heaven" (Acts 1:11).

Anything finished holds little interest. If we could only look back and see that Jesus had finished up the faith in the first century, we might be prone to say, "Ho hum! Jesus was on earth once with James and John, but that's all past now. It must have been nice back in the good old days when things were really popping."

But Jesus is just as much our contemporary as he was the contemporary of Matthew, Mark, Luke, and John. In fact, we may get to see what they only dreamed about. Jesus is coming again! And we may get to see this cloud-splitting finale any day!

What shall we do in the meantime? Shall we find ourselves crying, "We sure wish we could have seen Jesus when he came around the first time?" No, never! We indeed shall see him. Every eye shall see him! Then we who stand at the end of Christianity will see that we were just as much participants in the life of Christ as those who knew him in the flesh. Some—like the magi—will have seen him when he was just a baby. Others like the apostles will have seen him in his mature ministry. Some, perhaps us, will have seen him—the Christ triumphant, the Lord of our fortunate era—settling down from heaven into our own times.

PRAYER
Lord, I long to see you, to behold what all the ages have dreamed about. Come quickly and make us the great crowd who behold and understand the Christ of power and his great church triumphant.

CHAPTER THIRTY-ONE

RESURRECTION MORNING

On the first day of the week, very early in the morning, they came to the tomb, bringing the spices they had prepared. [2] They found the stone rolled away from the tomb. [3] They went in but did not find the body of the Lord Jesus. [4] While they were perplexed about this, suddenly two men stood by them in dazzling clothes. [5] So the women were terrified and bowed down to the ground.

"Why are you looking for the living among the dead?" asked the men. [6] "He is not here, but He has been resurrected! Remember how He spoke to you when He was still in Galilee, [7] saying, 'The Son of Man must be betrayed into the hands of sinful men, be crucified, and rise on the third day'?" [8] And they remembered His words.

[9] Returning from the tomb, they reported all these things to the Eleven and to all the rest. [10] Mary Magdalene, Joanna, Mary the mother of James, and the other women with them were telling the apostles these

things. [11] But these words seemed like nonsense to them, and they did not believe the women. [12] Peter, however, got up and ran to the tomb. When he stooped to look in, he saw only the linen cloths. So he went home, amazed at what had happened.

THE EMMAUS DISCIPLES

[13] Now that same day two of them were on their way to a village called Emmaus, which was about seven miles from Jerusalem. [14] Together they were discussing everything that had taken place. [15] And while they were discussing and arguing, Jesus Himself came near and began to walk along with them. [16] But they were prevented from recognizing Him. [17] Then He asked them, "What is this dispute that you're having with each other as you are walking?" And they stopped walking and looked discouraged.

[18] The one named Cleopas answered Him, "Are You the only visitor in Jerusalem who doesn't know the things that happened there in these days?"

[19] "What things?" He asked them.

So they said to Him, "The things concerning Jesus the Nazarene, who was a Prophet powerful in action and speech before God and all the people, [20] and how our chief priests and leaders handed Him over to be sentenced to death, and they crucified Him. [21] But we were hoping that He was the One who was about to redeem Israel. Besides all this, it's the third day since these things happened. [22] Moreover, some women from our group astounded us. They arrived early at the tomb, [23] and when they didn't find His body, they came and reported that they had seen a vision of angels who said He was alive. ²⁴ Some of those who were with us went to the tomb and found it just as the women had said, but they didn't see Him."

²⁵ He said to them, "O how unwise and slow you are to believe in your hearts all that the prophets have spoken! ²⁶ Didn't the Messiah have to suffer these things and enter into His glory?" ²⁷ Then beginning with Moses and all the Prophets, He interpreted for them in all the Scriptures the things concerning Himself.

²⁸ They came near the village where they were going, and He gave the impression that He was going farther. ²⁹ But they urged Him: "Stay with us, because it's almost evening, and now the day is almost over." So He went in to stay with them.

³⁰ It was as He reclined at the table with them that He took the bread, blessed and broke it, and gave it to them. ³¹ Then their eyes were opened, and they recognized Him; but He disappeared from their sight. ³² So they said to each other, "Weren't our hearts ablaze within us while He was talking with us on the road and explaining the Scriptures to us?" ³³ That very hour they got up and returned to Jerusalem, and found the Eleven and those with them gathered together, ³⁴ who said, "The Lord has certainly been raised, and has appeared to Simon!" ³⁵ Then they began to describe what had happened on the road, and how He was made known to them in the breaking of the bread.

THE REALITY OF THE RISEN JESUS

³⁶ And as they were saying these things, He Himself stood among them. He said to them, "Peace to you!" ³⁷ But they were

startled and terrified, and thought they were seeing a ghost. [38] "Why are you troubled?" He asked them. "And why do doubts arise in your hearts? [39] Look at My hands and My feet, that it is I Myself! Touch Me and see, because a ghost does not have flesh and bones as you can see I have." [40] Having said this, He showed them His hands and feet. [41] But while they still could not believe for joy, and they were amazed, He asked them, "Do you have anything here to eat?" [42] So they gave Him a piece of a broiled fish, [43] and He took it and ate in their presence.

[44] Then He told them, "These are My words that I spoke to you while I was still with you, that everything written about Me in the Law of Moses, the Prophets, and the Psalms must be fulfilled." [45] Then He opened their minds to understand the Scriptures. [46] He also said to them, "This is what is written: the Messiah would suffer and rise from the dead the third day, [47] and repentance for forgiveness of sins would be proclaimed in His name to all the nations, beginning at Jerusalem. [48] You are witnesses of these things. [49] And look, I am sending you what My Father promised. As for you, stay in the city until you are empowered from on high."

THE ASCENSION OF JESUS

[50] Then He led them out as far as Bethany, and lifting up His hands He blessed them. [51] And while He was blessing them, He left them and was carried up into heaven. [52] After worshiping Him, they returned to Jerusalem with great joy. [53] And they were continually in the temple complex blessing God.

The Ascension

Up he goes! The Christ, white-robed, is leaving earth. He is dressed formally for his return, which may occur at any moment.

Watch him rise in power! See him sever gravity and cut the cords that bind us, his watchers, to our dull earth. The heavens do indeed proclaim the glory of God, and all that vast cathedral ceiling we call sky, exists to frame a single ornament, the rising Savior.

Rub your eyes to hold as long as you can, the ever-rising vision. A speck of searing white, flying out against the burning blue.

See, He is still there! He is all but gone. So small a thing—a glorious, white period on the blue parchment of God's heaven.

Now we see . . . now not quite . . . now he is gone! The grand era of Incarnation has been swallowed by the sky to set the world to watching.

Rembrandt utilizes the traditional symbolism associated with divine presence, offering a stark contrast between heavenly light and earthly darkness. Christ stands cruciform, revealing the wounds in his hands, bathed in the light of God's glory.

This is the disciple who testifies to these things and who wrote them down. We know that his testimony is true. And there are also many other things that Jesus did, which, if they were written one by one, I suppose not even the world itself could contain the books that would be written.

—THE GOSPEL OF JOHN
CHAPTER 21, VERSES 24-25

Your Own
Eyewitness Testimony

Because these first-century eyewitnesses were faithful to record what they saw, heard, and experienced as they walked with Christ, we have the privilege of being there with them – of hearing His words echo across the centuries and into our living rooms. In fact, our very lives may be the debt we owe them for being obedient to God in writing their Gospel histories, for through their faithful retellings we have seen Christ face to face and have been drawn by the Holy Spirit into relationship with Him.

Written words have a lasting impact.

So we offer you these pages in this special book about Jesus Christ's life and ministry to record your own eyewitness testimony – to recall the people, places, and events God used to turn your heart to Him, to recapture the benchmark moments when His patience outlasted your persistence, to reflect on all the times when fear came into play but faith still won the victory.

Something you've come across in reading this book may even have stirred a new discovery about Him in your heart and mind. Write it down. You or someone you love may need it later.

Could it be that your willingness to put your own experience with Christ into permanent ink will stir another heart generations away? They may come across this volume on a dusty bookshelf or in a forgotten storage box, read the words of one who knew Him personally, and either find their faith renewed or find the Friend who sticks closer than a brother.

For we serve a living God, a risen Savior, an eternal King. And like those who walked with Him in Galilee, you have walked with Him in your own time and space. Your story begs to be told. It is like no other.

Will you share it so that others may walk with Him, too?